Tool Kit for Trainers

Tool Kit for Trainers

A Compendium of Techniques
for Trainers and Group Workers

Tim Pickles

FISHER
er
BOOKS™

Copyright © 1996 by Tim Pickles
The moral right of the author has been
asserted.
First published in Great Britain in 1995 by
Gower Publishing, Ltd., Aldershot, Hampshire

North American edition published by
Fisher Books
4239 W. Ina Road, Suite 101
Tucson, Arizona 85741
(520) 744-6110

Printed in USA
Printing 10 9 8 7 6 5 4 3 2 1

Publishers: Bill Fisher
Howard Fisher
Helen V. Fisher

North American Editor: Sarah Trotta
U.K. Editor: Jane Moody

Cover Design: Performance Design
Book Production: Deanie Wood
Randy Schultz

**Library of Congress
Catalog-in-Publication Data**

Pickles, Tim, 1952-
    Tool kit for trainers: a compendium of
techniques for trainers and group workers
/ Tim Pickles.
        p. cm.
    ISBN 1-55561-112-5
    1. Employees--Training of--Problems,
exercise, etc. 2. Group relations training--
Problems, exercises, etc. I. Title.
HF5549.5.T7P445 1996
658.3' 124--dc20   96-26045
                                                CIP

Acknowledgment: Some of the ideas presented in the section "Confronting Resistance" are
derived from work presented by Peter Block in *Flawless Consulting* (Learning Concepts, 1987).

Contents

Acknowledgments

In devising this *Tool Kit*, I have drawn upon the work and experience of many past and present colleagues, to whom I owe a great debt. The origin of many techniques and exercises is often buried in history. Where a source is known, I have acknowledged it, but, where I have omitted to give credit to someone's original work, I apologize in advance.

I wish to express my thanks to Alex Stevens, Bruce Britton, Lesley Greenaway, Phil Hope, John Holt, Art Schindler, Moira Halliday, Barry Hope, Alan Brown, Peter Block, Sarah Hargreaves, Peter Honey, Howie Armstrong, Allan Brown, Penny Sharland, Dave Francis, Warren Feak, Bill Kitson and Donna Brandes — all of whom provided source ideas for techniques which have found their way into this *Tool Kit*. I trust I have not misrepresented their work.

Dedication

For Sarah, Phil, Moira and Penny —
a group who offer me so much learning.

Chapter 1

Introduction to the *Tool Kit*

This *Tool Kit* began with my own hunt for a manual that would expand my personal repertoire of activities and methods to use with training and development groups. Over the years, I have picked up a range of techniques from watching colleagues, from participating in groups and from experimentation in my own groups. I knew there must be more because there were still many group situations in which I did not feel comfortable. As time went on, I found a range of textbooks and manuals that described particular applications — role-play, creative games, self-assessment exercises and so on — but none that provided me with an overall digest of methods that I could dip into when required.

Like many trainers, I started to acquire exercises, worksheets and activities from different sources. The key for a trainer is never to throw away any of this material. It takes time to sort and file it so the right technique can be retrieved when required. In many instances, the exercise needs to be amended from its original format to suit the new purpose, but its essence remains recognizable. Such a library of methods and techniques became known as the *Tool Kit*. Like the bag of household tools, it gathers together in one place a wide diversity of instruments and devices for tackling common situations. Some of the tools may be used rarely or never and find their way to the bottom. Others are old and trusted favorites, which are in constant use because they can be relied upon to solve a problem. For most collectors, there is a sense of excitement in finding a new tool — or technique — and adding it to their tool kit. New techniques are used warily and tested. If useful, they join the established repertoire. Otherwise they are kept "just in case" rather than being discarded.

That is the idea behind this *Tool Kit*: to provide in one volume a stimulating and challenging variety of methods for use with a wide range of training and development groups. Most users will find familiar activities in these pages. I hope you will also find brand-new ones, and improved reworkings of others that may not have inspired confidence when you first saw them.

This is a tool kit to dip into selectively. You may want to use it to expand your own range of techniques. Others may wish to have it as a backup resource when working with groups, to provide ideas when the program is not working as planned. No tool kit can be comprehensive in its coverage. There are gaps and omissions in this catalog that reflect my own areas of inexperience. Similarly, most of these techniques are capable of almost infinite adaptation. Only a few variations can be described in the text, which inevitably concentrates on the basic uses of each technique. You are warmly encouraged to take these technique descriptions as starting points for your own work and to adapt and refine them to suit your own working context.

Training and Group Work

The *Tool Kit* is addressed equally to trainers and group workers. The language of both disciplines is used interchangeably throughout. I view the areas of work as very similar. The good trainer uses his or her experience of group-work processes to make the course more dynamic. The competent group worker recognizes that many groups exist to enable their members to develop or learn something new for themselves.

The conceptual philosophy underpinning the approach and techniques advocated here is based upon the cycle of experiential learning. People's learning starts from personal experience, whether from real life or artificially generated in the group. They need opportunities to reflect on before generating conclusions and theories, which can then be tested in the real world through further experience.

These *Tool Kit* techniques are devices either for focusing attention and aiding reflection as people come together to examine their own experiences, or for generating artificial experiences within the group for study. Do not regard the techniques as ends in themselves, to be used and discarded as stand-alone events. Use them as a means by which individuals and groups are helped to develop their own learning and insights.

These techniques are particularly appropriate with several types of groups:

- **Training groups,** in which participants are engaged in developing awareness, knowledge or skills to apply in their work or lives.

- **Personal-development groups,** a particular form of training group in which members define their learning needs for themselves and then collaborate to support each other in achieving them.

- **Task-based groups,** whose members are engaged in planning and implementing some new initiative.

- **Problem-solving groups,** in which people come together with the specific aim of defining and resolving a current difficulty.

- **Team-development groups,** in which colleagues who work together for some or all of their time meet to improve their own collaborative functioning.

- **Mutual-support groups,** whose membership is defined by some common experience resulting in a need for sharing and support from each other, often without the direction of a formal leader.

All of the models and techniques in this *Tool Kit* have been tested and used in some or all of these different types of training, development and support groups.

Definitions

Training and group-work manuals are often full of jargon. While I try to avoid unnecessary language, some common words and phrases are required to make the text easier to understand. As far as possible, these are consistent throughout the *Tool Kit*.

Each method introduced in the manual is described as a *technique*. When techniques are applied in the context of a specific training event, they are usually referred to as an *exercise* or *activity* denoting the task-centered focus of the event. A series of such exercises run over a day or half-day may be known as a *session*: This corresponds with common practice among leaders and trainers for planning work around discrete sessions. Where several sessions are run with the same group, the complete package is referred to as a *program*.

The training or group *program*

↓

may consist of several *sessions*

↓

each of which may involve different *activities* or *exercises*

↓

and each activity requires an appropriate *technique*

The people who have responsibility for organizing and running sessions are variously described as *trainers, group leaders, tutors* and *facilitators*. Although each may operate in a different context, this *Tool Kit* is designed to show that they employ basically similar skills and methods when working with groups of people. The text interchanges the use of each of these terms and the user is invited to substitute his or her own self-descriptions as necessary.

Those who take part in a training or development group are referred to as *participants* or *group members*. Again, the phrasing is designed to be interchangeable.

To avoid repetitive use of the cumbersome phrase "his or hers," the gender pronouns used in descriptions of each technique sometimes make the trainer a woman and at other times a man. The same applies to participants, though usually they are made the opposite sex of the trainer in that section. Throughout the *Tool Kit*, the sexes are represented equally in both roles.

As trainers and group workers, we must remain aware of issues relating to power and social equality. It is all too easy to abuse the power that is conferred (or grasped) by those with some responsibility for leadership. (This issue is explored in Chapter 2.) The sensitive group leader will also be aware of differences in expectations and ways of thinking created by the race, gender, sexuality, disability and cultural background of participants. These factors influence how people react to each other. The leader needs to devise ways of working that empower all participants in their fields of work.

A Guide to the Layout

The *Tool Kit* is divided into straightforward chapters. After this introduction, Chapter 2 provides some simple models for understanding work with a wide range of groups. This is not a comprehensive description of group work, but rather a series of short explanations designed to help the practitioner *think* about work with groups. Each model is based upon the notions of experiential group work described earlier. Each model is illustrated with a diagram. Each of the model descriptions can be used in various ways: as background reading, as a reminder of key points, and as notes the trainer may need to give participants about learning and development processes.

Chapter 3 introduces nearly 40 different techniques, activities and exercises for use with training and development groups at different stages. Where appropriate, these are cross-referenced to the models described in Chapter 2. Each technique is described in its own section using some or all of a series of standard headings, outlined below:

Purpose	An introductory paragraph sets out what the technique is designed to achieve and gives an indication of how it might be used in practice.
Method	This paragraph usually provides detailed instructions about how to set up and run the technique. It includes warnings about pitfalls and how to avoid them. A step-by-step approach makes the technique easy to follow. When the technique encompasses a series of related exercises, each of these is given a separate subparagraph.
Examples of the Technique	Most techniques are illustrated by examples of when and where they might be used in practice. The examples are deliberately drawn from a wide range of training and development groups.
Worksheet or Handout	You may copy and amend some worksheets or handouts provided in this manual as necessary. These worksheets illustrate the method in practice and make it easier for the user to take and apply the idea. See photocopying permission, page iv.
Possible Variations	The previous paragraphs describe how the basic technique works. Here, suggestions are offered about how the technique can be refined, extended or varied to meet different purposes or audiences.
Suitability	A concluding paragraph usually sums up the scope of each technique with comments about its ease of use, the type of audience with which it works best, or when it might best be used.

Each of the tools in Chapters 3, 4 and 5 is also given a risk factor. This is a score ranging from one to five that indicates how risky and revealing the activity may appear to participants.

- *Low risk-factor scores* mean that little participation is required, or that participants have a very high degree of personal control over what they reveal.

- *High risk-factor scores* indicate techniques that require very careful introduction by the leader and a high degree of trust among group members.

The most powerful techniques tend to be those with a high risk factor; these activities can provide the greatest opportunities for learning. Risk scores are inevitably generalized, but they help indicate the relative difficulty of each technique.

Chapters 4 and 5 provide more techniques to use with groups. Chapter 4 lists techniques that help evaluate the work of any group, while Chapter 5 suggests methods by which people who wish to co-train or co-lead a group can prepare themselves for working together.

Chapter 6 provides an overview of things that can go wrong in different group situations and offers help in detecting and analyzing such problems. In the spirit of group work, the responsibility for solving difficulties is shared between the trainer and group members. This chapter sets out some methods the trainer can use to encourage the group to confront its resistances.

Building Your Own Tool Kit

Collecting and collating these techniques over the past few years has been fun for me. This cannot be a definitive tool kit because each trainer and group worker has his or her own variations and favorites, and new ones are being invented all the time. If using this manual leaves you with only one idea, I hope it is to start organizing your own personal tool kit. This involves building a databank of ideas, exercises, worksheets, pictures, instruction lists, videos — anything you use with courses and groups — in a format that works for you and enables easy retrieval. You will develop some materials yourself; many others will come from colleagues, friends, TV programs, conferences, workshops and other places. Organizing them is a job in itself. I know people who use filing cabinets, computer disks, bookshelves and ring binders. There are many ways of cataloging such materials. Each trainer needs to devise a personal system that works effectively.

There are two tips that I have found useful in building my tool kit. The first is to keep it simple. This phrase, the basis of several acronyms at work, applies at many levels. Tool Kit systems need to be simple if they are to work conveniently. More important, the best techniques are often the simplest. Complex techniques take longer to explain and increase the chance that people will misunderstand instructions. A simple technique is usually both neat and effective.

The second tip is to use graphics rather than words wherever possible. A picture tells a thousand words! The essence of our work is to help people understand and learn, and providing them with clear visual images of the main points will always enhance their recollection of the event.

Chapter 2
Models for Understanding Groups

Group work theory is well covered in a number of textbooks. Rather than repeating this material, I will present in this chapter several short sets of notes that outline critical points about working with any sort of training or learning group. These notes can be used in a variety of ways.

- The individual reader can use them for self-study.

- The trainer can use them as notes when teaching about groups.

- They can be copied and issued as reference handouts (see photocopying notice, page iv).

- They can be kept close at hand and referred to if difficulties are encountered during a session.

The Cycle of Experiential Learning

Model

People learn from experience. This model was first expounded by Kolb and has since been widely recognized in many of the standard texts about training and learning. Few people can learn new material in an abstract context without some reference to their own knowledge and experience. Kolb recognized the cyclical pattern in which people undertake new learning. He showed it in a simple diagram:

Experience of events in the real world

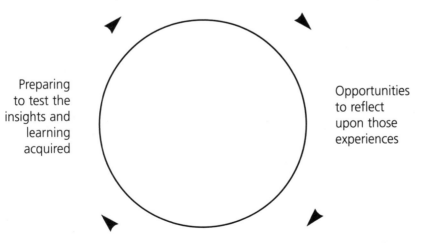

Preparing to test the insights and learning acquired

Opportunities to reflect upon those experiences

Drawing generalizations and conclusions from such reflection and creating theories and models to explain them

Kolb, D. (1984): Experiential Learning, *Prentice Hall.*

This cycle of learning involves four sequential steps:

- **Experience.** All learning begins with some experience: of an event, incident or occurrence. This may be naturally occurring, as with most life experiences, or artificially created, as for instance, when the trainer introduces a role-play into a course.

- **Reflection**. Awareness and personal learning start when people have opportunities to reflect on the experiences they have gained. This can be enhanced if the facilitator provides helpful structures for reflection.

- **Drawing conclusions.** Reflection leads to a sorting and understanding of earlier experiences from which the person can draw conclusions and generalizations. These help order the experiences and provide a framework in which to learn about them.

- **Testing.** Using this framework, new experiences can be planned that test the conclusions, either to confirm the learning already achieved or to generate more evidence. Such testing leads to more experiences in the real world, which set the cycle in motion again.

This simple model is the basis for much experiential training and group work. It underpins several of the models that follow in this chapter and forms a foundation for the successful introduction and use of the techniques throughout this *Tool Kit*.

Five-stage Model of Group Development

The life and development of any group, no matter what its purpose, is *not* random. There is a structure and sequence to its evolution. By understanding this sequence, and recognizing when each of the stages is occurring, the trainer or group worker is better prepared to work with the group and introduce suitable material at an appropriate time. Many of the problems that occur during a training session can be attributed to different members of the group (including the trainer or leader) believing or thinking that the group has reached a different stage.

One of the easiest ways of looking at a group (and the simplest to remember) is through a five-stage model. The model suggests that all groups go through five steps, which evolve one from another. These steps are described below.

Forming: The group comes together and establishes an initial pattern.

Storming: Members of the group resolve the purpose of and roles in the group.

Norming: Agreement is reached about how the group will work.

Performing: The group works on its task or function.

Mourning: The group prepares to end.

At each stage, the task of the group is different and the processes operating within the group vary considerably. The concept is illustrated in the chart on page 11.

Moving from one stage to the next is not automatic. Many events within the group can trigger a change in the pattern. Some examples include:

- Adding new members to the group, when the group must return to forming.

- A struggle for influence between two group members, when the group is thrown back to storming.

- A loss of direction or purpose while engaged in the task, when the group must return to norming.

- A reluctance to end the group, leading to sabotage and proposals for an extension, which may return the group to storming.

As a result many groups are forever jumping back one or two stages before returning to their task. If you could "map" the progress of the group through the five stages against time, you might end up with a chart something like the one below.

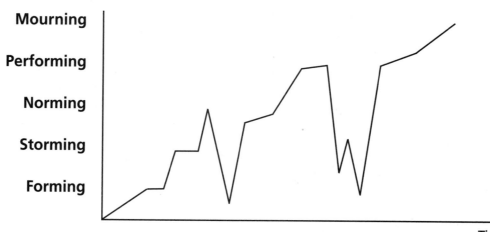

Group Development over Time

One factor that complicates this simple model—and often leads to conflict or storming within the group—is that participants are themselves at different stages. One person may be clear about the purpose of the group and its rules, and be impatient to get on with the task. Another person may be far less sure what the aims of the group are, whether it is the right group, and whether to stay. This person has not reached norming. Classic difficulties arise when a group has been performing well for some time but two new participants join. While some are anxious to stay performing, the group must return to forming if the new members are to be successfully integrated.

One of the key functions of the trainer or group leader is to keep track of what stage the group has reached and then help people move on. For success, the group can only move forward through these stages at the speed of the slowest member. Managing the frustrations of those who wish to move faster is part of the trainer's role.

A feature of many groups is the desire to start right into the task of the group—the performing stage. However, as this model demonstrates, participants must complete several important preliminary stages first. Unless this is done, the group runs the risk of breaking apart before the task has started. In a training context, this means paying attention to introductions, establishing the aims of the course and its boundaries, making people comfortable, and explaining procedures before starting the work of the course. Depending on the nature of the group, these early stages can take a substantial amount of time. There are no effective techniques for short-circuiting them without potentially compromising the outcome of the event.

Five-stage Model of Group Development

	Task of the group	Processes occurring
Forming	Introductions Coming together First agenda	Uncertainty Apprehension Excitement Enthusiasm Interest
Storming	Testing Breaking limits Challenges Walking out Nonparticipation	Fear Anxiety Loss of control
Norming	Reaching agreement Safeguards Defining the real agenda Acquiring skills Contracting	Relief Stability, certainty Commitment Negotiation
Performing	Undertaking the group task	
Mourning	Ending Leaving early Hanging on Forward planning Departing	Sadness Joy Celebration Regret Anticlimax Anticipation

Task versus Process

Model

There are two main aspects to the functioning of any training, personal development or organizational group:

- the task of the group, which defines what it aims to achieve, and

- the process of the group, which describes how it actually works.

Task and process are two sides of the same coin. Neither operates in isolation from the other. For the task-based goals of the group to be achieved, a suitable process method has to be chosen. Task and process drive each other.

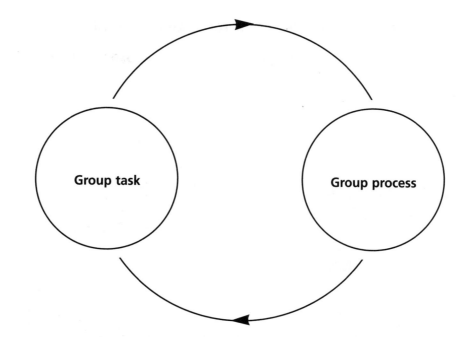

The task/process model

This task/process model of the group can be superimposed on the earlier five-stage model of the stages of a group's development, to illustrate how at different stages the relative importance of task and process varies. During forming, storming and mourning, *process* is dominant; during performing, the group's *task* comes to the fore. In the norming stage (reaching agreement about the group's goals and structures) task and process are probably in balance.

One of the most useful applications of the task/process model is in analyzing difficulties in the group. It is common to discover that problems arise when the trainer is addressing the process, while the participants wish to deal with the task, *or* the leader is promoting the task, but the participants are stuck in a process issue.

To illustrate, take the situation of a trainer introducing the group to a task-based activity when participants are resistant to the activity. The participants resist because they do not feel comfortable with each other (a process issue). Similarly, the group leader may be attempting to establish operating ground rules for the group but encountering difficulties because several participants are unclear about why the group is meeting (its task).

One way of looking for the cause of problems in any group is to quickly switch your attention from the current task or process (whichever is dominant at the time) to the other. This idea is pursued later in the section on **Working with Opposites** (see page 23).

Johari's Window

Johari's window identifies for participants some of the benefits of learning within a group. This simple model plots the knowledge and insights held by the individual against the knowledge and insights held by the rest of the group. In each case, some information is known by the respective participants and other information is not, as shown in a simple grid.

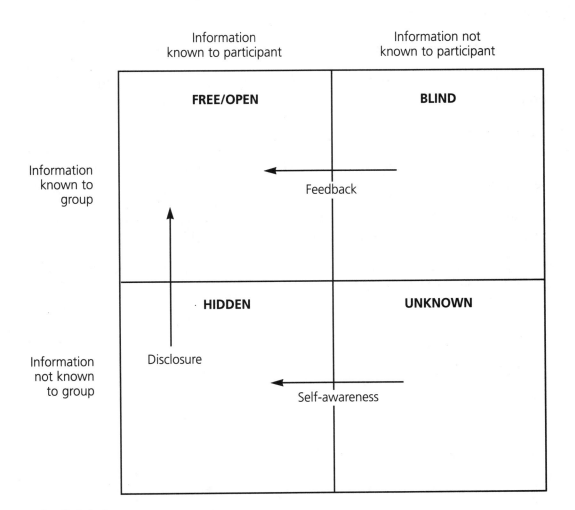

Johari's Window

In the process of working and learning together, some participants receive feedback from others and use it to discover more about themselves. Other participants are able to disclose to group members something they had previously kept hidden. Still other members may learn something about themselves through a growing self-awareness, even if they are not able to inform others.

Group Worlds and Real Worlds

One of the criticisms leveled at much work with groups is that what happens in any group is artificial and unrelated (or at best only hazily related) to events outside the group. Some groups may be divorced from the real world but, if so, their value is probably limited. In this context, the "real world" is defined as the work setting, family setting or other environment in which people live and work ordinarily; the "group world" refers to the conditions and operating rules that exist among members of the group when meeting together.

In working with any group, the trainer or group leader should seek to:

- bring material from the real world into the group for the group to consider and work with;

- use the group as an analogy of the real world;

- use the group as a "test laboratory" for skills and experience that can be used beyond the group;

- help members of the group take the learning and experience they derived from the group and transfer it to their lives or work in the real world.

These goals define the nature of the relationship between the group world and the real world and can be illustrated as follows:

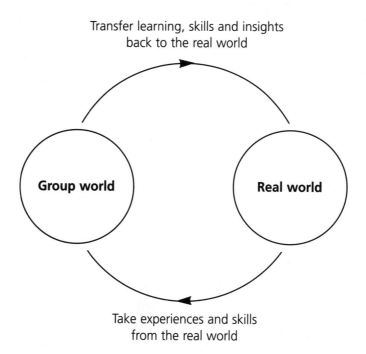

The relationship between the group world and the real world

In this way, while the group is itself different from the outside world, it draws upon the real world for its material, and the learning and products of the group are applied back in the real world.

Some people would argue that the dividing line between the two worlds is not as sharp as this because the group world is itself part of the real world. It may be more accurate to illustrate the process as shown in the diagram below.

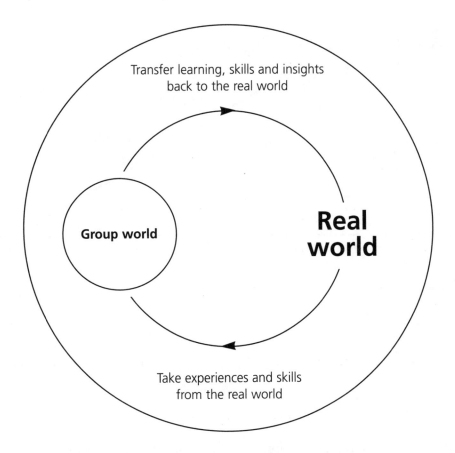

The relationship between the group world and the real world—alternative view

Risk versus Safety

Risk and safety are commonly regarded as opposites. If something is safe, there is little or no risk involved in doing it. On the other hand, if an activity is risky, there is usually a considerable danger attached to attempting it. Most people perceive a trade-off between safety and risk, which is shown diagramatically in the graph below:

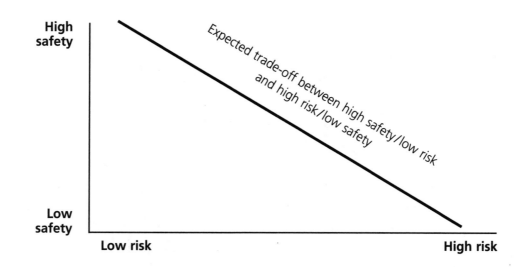

The safety-and-risk trade-off

In running any group, the trainer or group leader has to overcome this apparent trade-off.

Groups often have two requirements to be effective:

- They need to be safe, so that people are willing and able to participate.

- They should invite people to take risks and experiment to expand their learning and awareness within the group.

The trainer must create an environment that is both safe and conducive to risk-taking. Members join the group with little awareness of how it functions: At that point it is not particularly safe and they are willing to risk little. As the group develops, the task of its leader is to create an environment that is increasingly safe, secure and trusting so that all participants are encouraged to take greater risks in their own contribution and development:

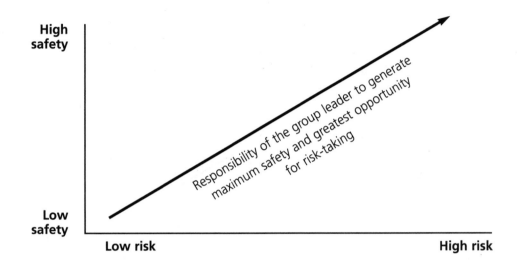

The safety-and-risk trade-off (developing group)

The methods by which the group leader can accomplish this involve:

- negotiating a set of ground rules for the group, which are agreed to by all members;

- allowing an increasing sense of direction and control over the work of the group to be transferred to its members as time develops;

- acting in a supportive and facilitative way so that members feel encouraged to attempt new things;

- minimizing the distractions and interruptions from outside the group;

- remaining alert to processes and feelings within the group and intervening to tackle problems when necessary.

The Power Ball

Following the action in any sort of group can be difficult. Even the most experienced facilitator sometimes gets caught up in group processes and loses sight of the overall direction, or fails to notice key changes happening in the way the group is working. Often, it is necessary to stand back and take a more detached view of what is going on.

One of the most instructive ways of doing this is to map the power structure within any learning or development group. This activity is based on a simple idea. At any time, the attention of the group is directed towards one person (occasionally two). At that moment, this person has "power" in the group because she is exercising some control or influence over the others. Such authority is gained in all sorts of ways, including:

- speaking to the rest of the group

- acting aggressively

- having an emotional outburst

- asking a question

- remaining silent

- standing up (when everyone else is sitting down)

- engaging in a private conversation with a neighbor

- heckling

- writing the notes

These actions do not always result in the individual gaining authority, because this depends on the personality of the individual and the circumstances of the event. However, they can be a good indicator of someone making a "power play."

By referring to "power" in this way, I do not want to suggest the action is necessarily bad or unwanted. At any one moment, *someone* needs to be leading or influencing the group, or the group's tasks would never be achieved. Using the idea of power or authority is a convenient way of directing attention towards the participants who are driving events in the group at that moment. As we shall see, the source of that power will frequently change around the group.

Mapping or tracking the location of that power involves focusing on an imaginary ball in the group. Whoever has control at any moment has the ball. The ball may be passed to someone else (for example, when a question is asked), or the ball may be taken by someone else (for example, by standing up or creating a distraction). Remaining detached and following the movement of this imaginary ball will tell you a great deal about the functioning of the group.

You can track the power ball mentally or by jotting down where it is moving over a few minutes. One such note is shown below.

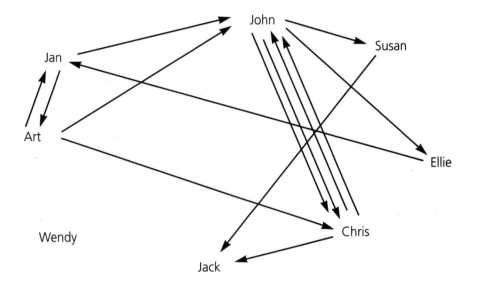

Tracking the power ball

Tracking the power ball enables you to see who has most authority, who communicates with whom, whether people are receivers or transmitters of comments, and who is apparently weakest in the group.

Such observation relies upon a detailed analysis of the minutiae of group processes. Sometimes, important changes in power are signalled by no more than a sideways look, a discreet cough, or a single word. Mapping helps you to look at these small gestures as well as the lengthy speeches or grand gestures that so often appear to occupy the time of the group but which, in reality, may have little influence. This is the microbehavior of the group. Such microbehavioral gestures frequently determine what is happening in the group.

Power and Authority in Groups

It is rare to work with a group in which everyone is equal. Even if participants are technically of the same status, people operate in different ways to achieve more or less personal authority. Thus, a dominant or assertive person exercises an influence over the group, while a retiring person effectively abdicates some personal authority to others. In any training or development group, the trainer is likely to have more authority by virtue of his or her status: Participants expect the trainer to be more knowledgeable, more skilled, or more responsible. In other groups, this authority is vested in the chair or person running the meeting.

As a rough rule of thumb, the greater the difference in authority between the leader and the participants in a group, the greater the perceived power of the leader; group participants are increasingly likely to follow the leader or abdicate responsibility to the leader's authority. This situation does not encourage motivation and learning among participants. Motivation and self-direction increase as participants gain control over their learning experience.

The dilemma for the trainer or group leader is, given the power and authority automatically vested in him by virtue of his status, how to increase the sense of responsibility and motivation among the participants so that they can take more control over their own learning. The trade-off is illustrated in the diagram below.

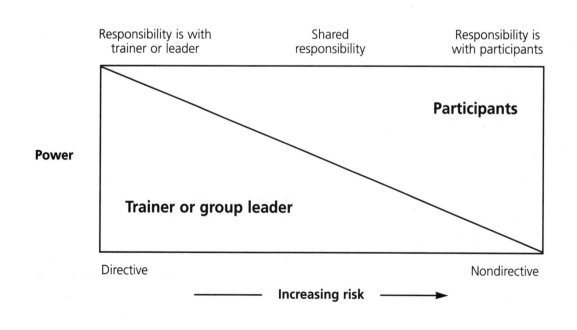

The power/risk dilemma

The model suggests that to increase the power of the participants in any group, the trainer or leader needs to act with a less directive style, offering participants choices and options. This style is likely to be more consultative and participative, so the learning becomes centered in the experiences and activities of the participants. The trainer or group leader shares power with participants as learning progresses under experimental methods.

Moving from trainer power to participant power involves increasing risk: the risk that things might go wrong, the group might not do what the trainer intends, or the original goals may not be met. These are genuine risks for the leader or trainer in choosing to share his power in the group. The gain, of course, is that the participants are likely to regard the process as more relevant and useful to them as they gradually assume ownership of the group's work.

In many situations, the leader will shift the balance of power as the group develops. In the early stages, the leader will retain almost 100% authority. This is often necessary when people are meeting for the first time, the purpose of the group is unclear, and participants have an expectation that the leader will take control. Later, as the group develops, this authority can be relaxed as members of the group are encouraged to take more responsibility for themselves. In effect, the group moves across the diagram on page 20 from left to right. Only when there is a crisis in the group might the leader or trainer want to reestablish more of his authority (although, at such times, some experienced leaders will attempt to hand even more responsibility to the participants).

The Doughnut Model

All training groups require boundaries within which to operate so participants know what is expected or permissible. Problems arise when not everyone is aware of the boundaries or when different people believe the boundaries to be in different places. One duty of the trainer is to make clear the actual boundaries for the group and to distinguish those aspects that are fixed and unchangeable from those that are more flexible. The doughnut model on the following page illustrates this clearly.

Examples of group aspects that could fall within the nonnegotiable part of the doughnut are:

- start and finish times;

- rules about physical safety;

- no-smoking policy.

Those aspects that are negotiable for some groups might include:

- the structure of group meetings;

- the frequency of meetings;

- how decisions are made.

All groups differ in the shape of their doughnut:

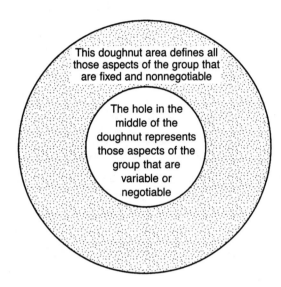

Some are tightly controlled, with extensive clearly defined boundaries and rules (large doughnut, small hole), while others are far more fluid, offering members plenty of opportunities to change the structure and nature of the group (large hole in relation to the overall doughnut).

In many groups, the doughnut shape will change over time. At the beginning, the boundaries are likely to be defined and relatively nonnegotiable. But, as the group gains confidence and experience, these controls can be relaxed and participants given more say in determining the boundaries. When control needs to be reasserted, the trainer may diminish the size of the hole to reestablish tighter boundaries or rules for the group.

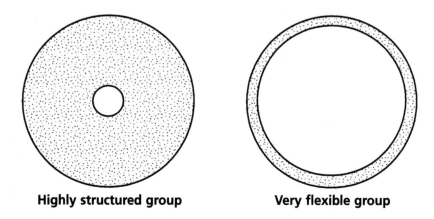

Highly structured group   **Very flexible group**

Working with Opposites

Working with groups is seldom easy. From the models and structures outlined already, it is obvious many things can go wrong! There is plenty for the trainer or group worker to keep an eye on. Usually, it is not possible to do all these things simultaneously. Working with a group is a constant process of making adjustments and changes as you go along—not sticking rigidly to a plan formulated in advance, particularly when that plan isn't working with the group.

Philosophers in ancient China explored the idea of *yin* and *yang*. Yin and yang represent the two halves of any dynamic interaction. The two are inseparable—one cannot occur without the other. Common examples of yin and yang are positive and negative, passive and active, female and male, dark and light.

This idea of interdependent halves can be applied to work with groups, particularly where problems or difficulties are occurring. The task-vs.-process model is one application of the concept. If the group has trouble with its task, work on process for awhile—and vice-versa.

The ability to change focus and work from another perspective is a critical skill for the trainer or group worker. It is most useful in dealing with problems and resistance that occur in the group. When combined with observational techniques the list below can help you decide what to do if things are not working: Try the opposite!

Task	<————>	Process
Work with the whole group	<————>	Divide into small groups
Leader control	<————>	Participant control
Active exercise	<————>	Passive exercise
Lecture	<————>	Activity
Stand	<————>	Sit
Talk	<————>	Draw
Sit in a circle	<————>	Sit in rows
Be directive	<————>	Be nondirective
Keep working	<————>	Take a break
Speak	<————>	Remain silent
Take part	<————>	Observe

Chapter 3
Tools for Learning

To work with training and other groups, you must devise and prepare a program that will achieve certain objectives. Most programs contain a range of components, each of which should fit together in a complementary way. To rely upon just one method for the program will induce boredom and disenchantment fairly quickly. The effective trainer and group leader needs access to a range of different techniques that can be used to vary the program style and tackle subjects through a range of stimulating approaches. This substantial part of the *Tool Kit* presents a catalog of different techniques.

It is impossible to identify every technique and variation in a directory of this type. This chapter aims to broaden your awareness of different techniques and to encourage experimentation and innovation. You are encouraged to use and adapt the exercises here to suit your audience and situation.

Much of the fun as a group leader and trainer comes from the unpredictability of the work: It requires creativity and flexibility to ensure a responsive approach that will make the best use of the learning opportunities available to participants through group work.

Action Plans

Purpose   Action plans are a way to convert the insights and learning acquired from a training course into real-world applications. They form an important part of the process for transferring the individual's work within the group to the external world outside the group.

Method   Action plans are usually designed as a short worksheet to suit a particular purpose. Many action plans are written by individuals or small groups as a record of how they intend to use the material in the future.

Tip: Use a series of headings or prompt questions on the action plans, as these can focus attention on particular areas for action appropriate to the circumstances.

Allow time for reflection and the completion of action plans toward the end of any training course or group. Pick the point at which no new material is to be introduced and when participants are considering how material that has been covered or discussed might be applied in their own settings.

Possible variations   An example of an action-planning worksheet is provided on the following page. An alternative is to encourage participants to make their own unstructured action-plan notes. One interesting way of doing this is to issue each person a blank memo sheet and envelope towards the end of the course. Time is provided for individuals to complete the memo sheet with ideas and plans for how they intend to use the course material in future work. The memo is addressed to its author. When the memo is finished, each person puts it into her envelope and adds her own name and address. The trainer collects the envelopes. The trainer explains that the simple act of writing the memo helps fasten the action plan ideas in each person's head—so they have no need for the written plan itself. However, because our commitment so often slips, the envelopes containing the original memo will be mailed by the trainer to the participants in two months' time as an "unexpected" reminder.

Suitability   Action plans are applicable in almost any situation in which participants have been involved in learning or discovery, and for which a period for reflection and application is made available, either during the event or shortly afterwards.

Action-planning Sheet

Name_____ **Date** _____

Course Title _____

My reasons for participating in this event were:

_____

_____

_____

The most important things I learned from this course are:

_____

_____

_____

What I have learned or discovered connects to my work in this way:

_____

_____

_____

The things that I now plan to start doing, or do more of, are:

_____

_____

_____

The things that I now plan to stop doing, or do less of, are:

_____

_____

_____

Other plans for action from this course are:

_____

_____

_____

I plan to review this plan of action on_____

Audio/visual Equipment

Purpose   Varied learning methods can be highly stimulating to any group. Modern technology need not be complex to operate and, by introducing relevant audio material or visual illustrations to a session, you may sustain the interest of the group longer. They may retain more, too.

Method   Several forms of audio or visual equipment are now readily available to groups. Most of these can be used in two different ways: as pre-created material that supports an input from the trainer, and as self-generated material, which the group itself compiles. Examples of different forms of audio and visual equipment and their uses are given below.

Examples of the technique

Technique	Prepared use	Group-generated use
Tape recorders	Prerecorded cassettes or radio programs to support a trainer presentation	Recording of counseling skills practiced by the group
Photographic slides	To illustrate points made by the trainer	To illustrate a project completed by participants
Overhead-projector transparencies	To support a prepared talk with graphics	To write on overlay sheets showing how a pattern or process might change over time
Video camera or camcorder; video recorder	To show a training video as part of a course	To record a role-play involving participants and for use in the subsequent debriefing
Personal computer	To use existing computer-based training programs to learn new skills or knowledge	To plan a complex project as part of a group task

A common experience of many trainers in using technological equipment is that either it does not work when you need it, or it works in a different way than expected. To avoid these potentially embarrassing problems, allow time to become familiar with and check the equipment before the session in which you will use it. The same applies to any prepared material or program that has been bought or rented. If at all possible, plan the session in such a way that it does not depend on the technology—so if it does fail, an alternative plan is ready to go.

Suitability Using different media can be an excellent way of maintaining a group's interest in a subject. However, there is a danger in using technology for its own sake and confusing the message. Before using any audio or visual equipment, ask yourself: "What will this equipment add to the session, and is it necessary for that purpose?" Only if you are convinced of its relevance should audio/visual equipment be regarded as suitable and useful for the group.

Brainstorming

Purpose

Brainstorms are a simple and effective method of generating ideas and suggestions. They are particularly effective when a subject is being introduced, or when group members lack confidence and wish to use each other as creative sources. The object of any brainstorm is to generate a quantity of ideas without regard to their quality; subsequent sorting and prioritizing of the ideas is needed to refine the raw results.

Method

An issue or question is defined and agreed upon. Members of the group, working together, are asked to suggest ideas, responses or possible solutions to the issue or question. These are recorded quickly on a flipchart. Every encouragement should be given to the rapid generation of responses so a steady stream of ideas develops quickly from the group. When this stream starts to dry up, the brainstorm can be brought to an end or another question asked.

When encouraging responses, several ground rules should be understood:

- Ideas and responses are accepted and recorded without comment.

- Evaluation and judgment of the responses is deferred until after the brainstorm is finished.

- Quantity is more important than quality of ideas.

- All responses are of equal merit during the exercise.

- One response can be used legitimately as a trigger for other responses.

The benefit of a brainstorm in any group is that a greater number of ideas, of a more varied nature, is generated by participants working together than by any one individual working on his own. The ideas from one person initiate or spark responses from another so the total list builds in a cumulative way.

Examples of the technique

Brainstorms are widely used as an introductory activity. Examples include:

- A product-development group generating ideas for the new product name

- A training group developing examples of specific problems prior to looking at ways of solving them

- A team listing possible solutions to an awkward situation

- Members of a group disclosing their reactions to a recent incident

Possible variations	Several variations of the basic brainstorm activity are possible by introducing a more structured approach to the exercise:

- From the first brainstormed list of problem solutions, select the most-likely and least-likely responses. Use each of these as a starting point to continue the same brainstorm. Using the *least-likely* response can be surprisingly creative because it invites participants to consider the original problem differently.

- Invite smaller groups of participants to work on the same brainstorm topic and compare results; this may lead to more diverse suggestions.

- Write several different but related issues on separate flipcharts and post these around the walls of the room. Give each participant a pen and ask everyone to respond to each sheet with suggestions. Participants may work on the sheets in any order and return to them as necessary.

Suitability	Brainstorms are an easy exercise that can be used with groups of all ages and abilities. Their best use is in introducing topics and issues and generating an initial interest in them before more detailed work is undertaken.

Cartoons

Purpose
When people meet in groups, they often demonstrate their verbal abilities to explain, describe and justify their positions on a topic. Verbal argument and discussion is often very helpful but it tends to rely on the analytical and rational part of the brain. Getting at a situation's subjective components, such as feelings, perceptions and attitudes, is more difficult. The creative tools of drawing and cartooning are one way around some of these problems. The phrase "a picture is worth a thousand words" sums up the advantage of these techniques. One diagram, drawing or cartoon can illustrate aspects of a situation that would take many words to convey. Cartoons are a type of drawing technique and they have a particular role in enabling us to explore situations and incidents.

Method
When a group wishes to focus on specific incidents or events, suggest producing a cartoon strip to highlight the main features. The cartoon strip takes the form of a storyboard of perhaps six to eight frames on a single sheet of paper or flipchart. These are numbered to show the sequence.

In the first storyboard frame, the opening situation of the incident is depicted. Key characters are shown, perhaps by stick-people symbols or quick sketches. Significant props or location identifiers are added to the drawing. Critical elements of the dialogue among characters are added in the form of balloons containing short summaries of what was said.

The second storyboard frame is completed in the same way, depicting the next significant event in the incident, again complete with characters, props and balloons. This process is repeated in successive frames until the incident ends. To focus on critical moments in the action may take between six and eight frames.

Stress several points when you introduce cartooning methods. The object is not to produce fine artwork but to capture the essence of the incident. Rough sketches are fine if they show what happened. Only critical points in the incident need to be recorded, not a complete script of everything that was said. There are no right or wrong ways of completing the cartoon, because the action is being described from the point of view of the contributors.

Cartoons. . .

The finished cartoon is just the starting point for an analysis of the event it depicts. Depending on the nature of the incident, the analysis could focus on several points:

- What did each character feel in each picture?
- Did characters act according to their feelings or were they influenced by some other pressure?
- At what point did the final outcome become inevitable?
- What could have been said, or done, and when, to change the outcome?
- What other courses of action were open to the characters?

Possible variations

Cartoons can be used in different ways. Once the incident has been depicted in a cartoon, the group can focus on alternative endings. To do this, participants should focus on specific frames and discuss how the action in that frame could have been different to bring about a different outcome.

For more adventurous groups, cartoons are a natural lead-in to role-plays, because the script has been generated and the key events are understood by all the participants. Turning the cartoon into a role-play enables practical rehearsal of skills and alternative actions to take place.

Suitability

Cartoons can work well with groups of all ages and abilities. Young people may be more willing to start drawing (adults can be inhibited by a self-perceived lack of drawing skills). To overcome potential difficulties, introduce the benefits of this technique and stress that the quality of the artwork is not being judged. With very reluctant groups, you may need to create the storyboard and add the drawings yourself in front of the group using the descriptions supplied by participants conversationally.

Use each frame of the storyboard to illustrate a key moment
in the incident. Use simple drawings to show the people and
events involved. Add "word balloons" or "thought balloons"
to show what each person was saying or thinking.

Case Studies

Purpose   Case studies are a method of providing examples of a subject, usually selected by the trainer or leader, for discussion and comment by the group. Case studies are chosen for their relevance to the issue under consideration and highlight specific aspects of the topic.

Method   As the name suggests, case studies may be used to depict examples of specific individuals, groups or families; particular problems; or a set of circumstances. Each case study describes one incident or event in some detail. The case study is often prepared on a handout so it can be copied and distributed to participants for discussion. The case study may contain a description of the event alone, or it may be supplemented with questions or pointers at the end to help to focus the subsequent discussion.

Case studies may be drawn from the trainer's own experience with the subject or from examples supplied by colleagues. In training events, some participants may have prior experience with the subject. You might ask them to prepare a case study from their own work in advance. Then use those case studies in the course. In some instances, case studies may be drawn from TV or video clips selected carefully to illustrate specific points. Case studies are usually based on real examples but it is possible, with care, to invent fictitious ones if the trainer has wide experience with the subject. One type of fictitious case study uses what-if methods to consider reactions to an event that might occur in the future.

Examples of the technique
- In training about management techniques, case studies of specific management problems are presented for group discussion.

- During discussion about personal values and beliefs, a participant offers a case study of an event to show how her values influenced the way she reacted to a situation.

- In making contingency plans for emergencies, case studies are invented to describe situations that might arise for the planners to consider on a what-if basis.

Possible variations   An alternative to case studies is to use real examples contributed by participants. They volunteer and discuss actual events in which they have been involved. For more details of this technique, see **Critical-incident Analysis** (page 47).

Suitability   Case studies are relatively easy to generate and simple to use. Most groups respond positively to case studies that are relevant to the subject. Their main limitation is that the event on which the case study is based may be beyond the direct experience of the participants, so the discussion can seem slightly abstract. To avoid this, use case studies contributed by the participants themselves, or try a critical-incident-analysis approach.

Checklists

Purpose

Checklists are a particular form of pencil-and-paper exercise similar to self-assessment sheets or questionnaires. They are used either to remind group participants of key points about a subject, or to enable them to rate themselves against some established criteria. Checklists serve as a useful reference point or as a way to summarize important factors being considered by the group.

Method

Most checklists are prepared by the trainer in advance. The checklist is similar to a shopping list; it lists headings and points in some sort of order, without going into detail. Each item on the checklist is self-explanatory and acts as a trigger or reminder to the reader of the arguments and explanation that underlie the point.

To be effective, checklists should not be too long, or they become a memory exercise. In many instances, between four and 10 checklist points are sufficient to act as a reminder.

Checklists may also act as a simple self-assessment sheet. Again, the analogy is to conventional lists. The user can "check off" items from the list that he has collected or completed. Sometimes items on a checklist may appear in a simple "yes/no" format; for example, when participants are assessing their abilities against a set of established criteria.

Examples of the technique

- After making a presentation on the future strategy for an organization's development to her staff, the director issues a checklist summarizing the targets that each senior manager is expected to work towards within the overall plan for the organization.

- Before running a role-play exercise with a group, an inexperienced trainer refers to a checklist of preparation and briefing points, to ensure he has prepared the group participants adequately.

- A staff group is considering the application of an equal-opportunities policy in their workplace. At the end of a session considering how the role of women in the organization might be given more recognition, the group prepares a checklist of action points for all staff members to carry out as part of their normal duties.

- A small agency is recruiting a new staff member. The selection group draws up a checklist of essential and desirable characteristics for their ideal candidate. After each applicant is interviewed, the selection group fills in a copy of the checklist to indicate whether the applicant possesses the characteristics.

Checklists. . .

Possible variations For more detailed ways of listing and assessing information, see **Self-assessment Activities** (page 123) and **Questionnaires** (page 97).
For more general comments about summarizing sheets, see **Handouts** (page 71).

Suitability It is often good practice to summarize the key points from a course in a checklist that participants can take home and refer to later.

Conflict-resolution Methods

7

Purpose

As we have seen from the five-stage model of group development in Chapter 2, conflict is inevitable in any group. Conflict may be overt or covert. Either way, unless it is dealt with and removed, the group's learning process is seriously impaired. Most arguments and conflicts are related to the particular context and focus of the group and have to be resolved within the group. While each such situation is unique, a number of approaches have worked in many groups. In this section, an outline provides simple techniques group leaders can use to help overcome conflicts. Use outlines as reminders both of what may have gone wrong and of how to move the group past the conflict.

Participant risk factor **4**

Method

Conflict-resolution approaches are grouped as:

Negotiable / Nonnegotiable

Where a conflict exists between members of the group and its leader, it may be that participants have lost sight of what is negotiable in the group, or that areas of discretion need to be renegotiated. The **doughnut model** from Chapter 2 offers an illustration of this. The leader can work with the group to restate those aspects of the group that were non-negotiable from the start and those areas over which the group has some discretion and control. A review of the "doughnut" reminds everyone of these areas and provides an opportunity for changing the boundaries if this is appropriate.

Ground Rules Revisited

Conflict sometimes arises because members of the group break the ground rules. Ground rules are those agreements and rules that group members establish at the "norming" stage for their own conduct. They may include factors that are negotiable with the leader. Broken ground rules can lead to conflict or withdrawal from the group of some members. While any member of the group is free to point out lapses, the group leader has a particular responsibility to monitor observance of the rules and to take action if they are not kept. When ground rules are broken, the group needs to be reminded of them and given an opportunity to discuss their continued relevance. Where conflict arises because ground rules are misunderstood or ignored, the group should be involved in reimposing them.

Alternating Viewpoints

Conflict between individuals can be heated. The dynamics of the argument may result in the more powerful protagonist dominating the discussion. But might is not necessarily right! In group-work terms, the leader must ensure that different points of view are protected and given equal attention. Where communication is becoming one-sided or overwhelming, a technique is required to balance the contributions. Structuring the different contributions so each person has the same amount of time to speak, refereed by the group leader, helps achieve this: One person is given five minutes of uninterrupted time, followed by the second; the first can then reply for a further five minutes, and so on. This technique protects each person's right to speak. The group leader has a responsibility to encourage open listening from the other participant because it is in the listening process that misunderstandings can be cleared up and different points of view respected.

Rounds

The use of a round is a way of extending the contributions to involve everyone in the group. Because conflicts tend to center on just two or three group members, they may occupy a disproportionate amount of the group's time. Calling for a round places this in perspective and enables other group members to comment. The technique is explained in more detail in the section on **Rounds** (page 115).

Finding Interests, not Positions

In most conflicts, participants adopt a position. They state their view or stance and then stick to it. The more they argue for it, the more defensive they become — and the more entrenched. They are unable to shift their position without losing face. Positions are not helpful to a conflict because they perpetuate it. Instead, as the leader or facilitator, you need to find the participants' *interests*. Interests are the concerns that underlie a position. To switch to interests, ask those in conflict "What is it about your position (or point of view) that is important to you?" By asking open-ended questions and allowing individuals to say more about *why* they hold their particular positions, the facilitator can build a picture of the underlying interests. When this is clearly understood, suggest, "So the most important concern for you is. . . ." Establishing the base concern enables group members to look for options that address that concern. Such options are likely to be more varied and numerous than the single position first identified. Discussion based upon different participants' interests offers scope for creativity in solving the problem.

Suitability   Conflict cannot be prevented, because it is often part of the process of defining what the group wishes to achieve. But neither can it be ignored. When conflict arises, it must be dealt with positively and constructively before the group can proceed further with its task. These techniques provide some openings for exploring what the conflict is about and how it can be resolved.

Creative Visualization

8

Purpose   Creative visualization involves the imagination. It occurs when a trainer invites group members to close their eyes and allow their minds to follow a story that she will relate. Creative visualizations are sometimes used as part of stress management and to encourage mental recall of earlier events.

Method   The trainer explains the process of the visualization and its purpose within the group. Sitting (or lying) comfortably, participants are asked to close their eyes and relax. You might suggest that people uncross their legs, put down papers and pencils, and loosen tight clothing.

In preparation for the exercise, you will need to know the outline of the story that is to be told. Some examples of the use of creative visualization with groups are provided below.

In a soft and reassuring voice, tell the story. This should be done slowly so that participants have plenty of time to hear what is said and form a mental picture of the evolving story. Most creative visualizations involve the listener as a player within the story. This is done by references to "you" and the things that "you" are doing. Occasionally, there may be silences to allow participants to imagine and mentally explore what is happening to them in the story.

The trainer should be the only person speaking. Everyone else should be asked to remain quiet throughout the exercise. The visualization works best if all external noises and distractions are eliminated.

As the story nears its end, let participants know. It may be appropriate to end with words such as: "This is a good point at which to end our story; when you are ready to come back into the group, open your eyes and make yourself comfortable; take as much time as you wish."

Some participants find the exercise difficult, embarrassing or uncomfortable. Do not force them to take part, but ask them to sit quietly to one side. If one or two people open their eyes during the visualization, ignore it by continuing with the story in a quiet and reassuring tone.

Examples of the technique   Creative visualization, sometimes known as *guided fantasy*, has a number of applications:

• Stress reduction

To reduce stress within a group, the trainer can develop a visualization in which participants are invited to mentally visit (or invent) a private beach with companions of their choosing. The story continues by asking people to think about the trees surrounding the beach, the weather, the sea and their activities on the beach. Instead of a beach, the visualization may be about an ideal house or other place where rest and relaxation are encouraged.

• Summary and recall

At the end of a training course, the trainer may use the creative-visualization technique to remind participants of all the events of the course by describing them in chronological order. Leaving silent spaces in the story invites participants to recall their contribution to that part of the course and their own learning. This activity reminds people about the material covered and helps reinforce it.

• Forward planning

By projecting events into the future, creative visualization encourages people to plan ahead. The story line may involve events expected to happen next week (or next month, and so on) and include references to the work of the group, so participants are invited to take that and apply it to their ordinary work in future.

Possible variations
Creative visualization is limited only by the ingenuity of the trainer in devising appropriate and relevant stories to use with a group in such an exercise.

Suitability
Although it seems somewhat strange to some participants, creative visualization can be a powerful way of encouraging recall and mental reflection. It requires the group to have a level of confidence and comfort with its own functioning, so the technique is more likely to be used in the later stages of a group's life. The trainer needs confidence in her ability to build and sustain the story over five or 10 minutes and to adapt the basic idea to include references to the work of that particular group.

Critical-incident Analysis

9

Purpose
Critical-incident analysis is a method of looking in detail at one specific event to draw lessons from the experience and make plans, if necessary, for skills, knowledge or behavior that may be required in the future. Critical-incident analysis is often used by individuals to reflect on their own experiences and learning. In a group or training context it can provide the focus for small-group work around identifying needs or problem-solving.

Method
Working as a small group, participants identify one or more actual events that are considered noteworthy because of their circumstances or their outcomes. While these events are likely to be typical of many other events, those chosen should be significant in the way they demonstrate or highlight the critical factors.

Each critical incident is then examined in turn. A brief description of the event is provided by the participants who were involved. Depending on the nature of the issue under review, the group may then explore several avenues, such as:

• How could this event have been prevented?

• How could a different outcome have been achieved?

• What additional skills or knowledge were required to achieve a different outcome?

• Why did the event proceed in the way that it did?

Critical-incident analysis can focus attention in various ways. The outcome depends on the aim of the exercise within the overall purpose of the group.

Example of the technique
In using critical-incident analysis, a prewritten schedule may help direct the attention of group members to specific points in their discussion. A simple worksheet of this type is provided on the next page.

Possible variations
With critical-incident analysis, examples are usually provided by participants themselves from their personal experience. For less experienced participants, a case-study approach with examples provided by the trainer or facilitator may be used.

Suitability
This technique requires participants to have some experience of the subject area, so that examples can be contributed easily. They should feel confident about examining examples of their own work, practice or behavior without undue threat from colleagues.

Critical-incident Analysis

Brief description of the event:

_____

_____

_____

_____

_____

What factors contributed most to the particular outcome of this event?

_____

_____

_____

_____

What **skills** or **knowledge areas** were needed to respond more effectively to this event? What **priority** would you attach to each (high/medium/low)?

Skills/knowledge   *Relative priority*

_____

_____

_____

_____

_____

How would you act differently in the future if this event happened again?

_____

_____

_____

_____

_____

Demonstrations

10

Purpose

Demonstrations are used whenever the trainer or leader wishes to show the group how something is done or what something looks like, without directly involving the participants. The technique leaves a high degree of control with the trainer.

Method

In a demonstration, the whole group observes the actions, methods or illustrations provided by one or two members of the group, usually involving or led by the group leader. The demonstration is what it suggests—an opportunity to view, but not take part in, the carrying out of a particular procedure or action.

Examples of the technique

Demonstrations may take several forms, of which the following are examples:

- In illustrating a particular skill or behavior, the trainer may provide a demonstration the rest of the group watches.

- When conducting an experiment, the trainer may ask the rest of the group to observe how it is done.

- Before the group undertakes a risky or dangerous exercise, the trainer may demonstrate how it should be carried out safely.

- When materials are scarce, a sample may be used in a demonstration so that the whole group can see the results without using large amounts of the materials themselves.

- When the materials or objects are impractical to bring to the group, the leader may select a demonstration in the form of pictures, slides or film to illustrate the originals.

Possible variations

One form of demonstration is commonly known as a *goldfish bowl* because of its similarity to people watching fish swimming in a bowl. Goldfish-bowl exercises often involve a demonstration role-play. Several members of the group, usually led or directed by the group leader, participate in a small role-play in the middle of the room, surrounded by nonparticipating members of the group who watch. This technique is helpful if several members are unwilling to participate because of the perceived risk or exposure involved.

Participant risk factor **1**

Suitability Demonstration methods tend to require a low degree of participation from the group members, while allocating most of the responsibility to the leader. This may be desirable when the leader wishes to retain control—for instance, if there is potential danger attached to the activity. If demonstration methods are appropriate but the trainer wishes to delegate this control to the group, an alternative is to ask one or more group members to undertake the demonstration. They may comply by means of a prepared case study, exhibition or other form of demonstration.

Dialog Books

11

Purpose

A dialog book is a technique that combines work in pairs with a sentence-completion exercise. The method prompts participants to consider and respond to various suggestions in a structured way, while working at their own pace.

Method

The dialog book consists of a series of sentence-completion statements, one statement to a page. The statements are arranged into an appropriate sequence, often with the least-threatening ones at the front (to draw participants into the exercise) and the more difficult or thought-provoking ones placed later in the book. Between 10 and 15 sentence pages are sufficient for most purposes. An introductory page containing instructions for the exercise goes at the front of the book and the pages are stapled together.

Participants work together in pairs. Each person has a copy of the dialog book. The instruction page is likely to say something like:

"This dialog book contains a series of half-completed sentences. Use them as prompts in the discussion with your partner. Read aloud the sentence printed on the page and add the ending that is most appropriate to you. Then discuss your sentence completion with your partner. When you have finished with a page, turn to the next. You and your partner should respond to alternate pages. Please take the pages in order and do not look ahead. You may skip particular pages if you wish.

If your partner has also finished reading these instructions, decide who will speak first and turn to the next page."

Examples of the technique

Dialog books can be used as an icebreaker exercise at the beginning of a course, or alternatively as a way of obtaining feedback and reflection at the end of a course.

As an icebreaker, sentences in the dialog book may take the form:

- The place where I normally work is...

- My main responsibilities are...

- My reasons for attending this course are...

As a reflection exercise, the sentences may be:

- The most useful part of this course for me was. . .

- Something I plan to do now is. . .

- The thing I regret about this course is. . .

Dialog books may be used to encourage discussion about the subject when it is being introduced for the first time:

- My own experience with this subject involves. . .

- The relevant skills I already possess are. . .

- An recent incident I found difficult was. . .

Possible variations

Variations of the technique can be found in the sections on **Sentence-completion Exercises** (page 127) and **Pairs** (page 85).

For an icebreaker exercise, vary the technique by asking participants to swap partners after every two pages of the dialog book, so they meet with different people in the group. This variation works best if you put a time limit on the discussion about each sentence, so participants finish at roughly the same time.

Suitability

Dialog books provide a semi-structured way of approaching a topic. The structure is provided by the nature and shape of the sentences contained in the book, over which the trainer has control. The informality of its use, with people working in pairs and able to determine their own level of disclosure on each topic, elicits a response from participants.

Diaries and Logs

12

Purpose The act of recording actions, events and thoughts is a useful method of encouraging reflection. Writing about something often takes more time than the original act, and this fact prompts the writer to think more carefully about how and why things occurred in the way they did. Logs and diaries are one way of encouraging this process.

Participant risk factor **2**

Method Course participants are asked to record their actions, thoughts or feelings in a written diary or structured log. The frequency of entries depends on the nature of what is being recorded. Logs can be kept at different times, as indicated below.

- **Pre-event logs** are a way of recording situations before the group meets. This is useful if case studies and examples are required for use by the group. Such logs also provide a measure of the "before-group" situation.

- **Event logs** are most often used for recording impressions and feelings as the event proceeds. These demonstrate reactions to group learning and can provide trainers with feedback.

- **Post-event logs** show how the content of a group or course is being applied subsequently. If the group is meeting on a series of occasions, the post-event log from one session is effectively the pre-event log for the next session, and provides a record of continuing learning.

Logs may be structured or unstructured. A structured log or diary focuses the writer's attention by using a series of predetermined prompts or questions to which the writer responds. This is most easily done by issuing participants a standard log sheet in a style similar to a questionnaire. An unstructured log or diary presents the writer with a blank space to fill in as he or she wishes.

Structured logs make it easier to compare entries, and give the person establishing the log's structure more control. This might be useful if, for instance, specific reactions or behaviors are being monitored. Unstructured logs give the writer more freedom and are particularly useful if feelings, attitudes and impressions are the subject of the log.

TOOLS FOR LEARNING

Diaries and Logs. . .

Examples of the technique

STRUCTURED LOG

Skill being practiced

....

Date

....

Describe the situation

....

How effective was your use of the skill in this situation?

....

How could you improve your use of this skill if the same situation were repeated?

UNSTRUCTURED LOG

Keep a note of the times and incidents when you are able to practice this skill. Record your feelings, thoughts and responses to each incident.

Possible variations

Rather than using a written log, group members could make an audio or video recording of events. While these may be more convenient, they do not encourage reflection in the same way, because they require less time. The way around this is to be sure that recordings are always played back at a later time and attention is paid both to the original event and to the reactions and responses of those listening to or watching the recording.

Suitability

Logs and diaries are a simple, inexpensive way of encouraging reflection. They need not take long to complete. They can be used by people of all ages and most abilities with relative ease.

Dilemma Boards

13

Purpose   This creative technique helps group members think about how they would respond to particular circumstances. It offers a realistic incident that might occur (or has) relevant to the issue being discussed in the group. It invites participants to say what they would each do, by choosing from among several options or selecting another course of action.

Method   Prepare a series of dilemma boards in advance. (A template worksheet is provided on page 57.) In the center square, a specific situation is described that poses a dilemma. In each of the four quadrants, an alternative or potentially realistic solution is described.

Participants work in small groups. Each small group is given copies of one or more dilemma boards.

One person in each group takes the first dilemma board, reads it aloud with the options, and suggests what she would do in response to that situation. Other participants may discuss the choice made. In many cases, the "best" response may be a combination of options—or one that is not identified on the sheet.

Other people in the group then take other dilemma sheets in turn.

In a plenary session, groups can be invited to compare responses, and the trainer can offer comment and advice where necessary.

Possible variations

- Instead of the dilemma boards being read aloud in a small group, they could be mounted on a wall, with participants invited to walk around and study the options. Having done this, each participant should write his name in one quadrant on each sheet to indicate the choice he prefers.

- Instead of preparing dilemma boards in advance, you could explain the technique and invite participants to generate their own dilemma situations and options for use by others in the group.

- An extended version of dilemma boards—which encourages greater reflection about the reason for choosing particular options—involves creating two "rings" of responses around the central dilemma. In the inner set of quadrant boxes, participants write what action they might take. In the outer quadrant boxes, they must provide a rationale for each suggested course of action.

- A variation of the basic theme is described in the section on **Situation Cards** (page 139).

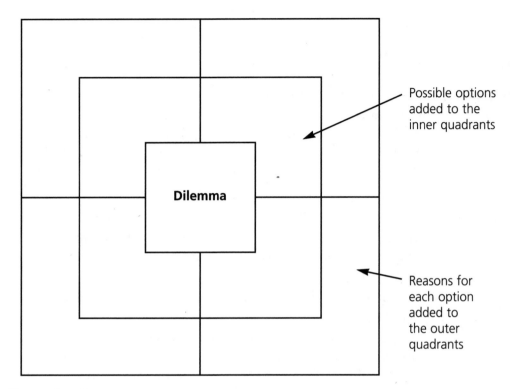

Possible options
added to the
inner quadrants

Dilemma

Reasons for
each option
added to
the outer
quadrants

The dilemma board

Suitability   Dilemma boards can be used wherever "what-if" situations are being discussed. It is useful for planning and rehearsing practical responses to such situations.

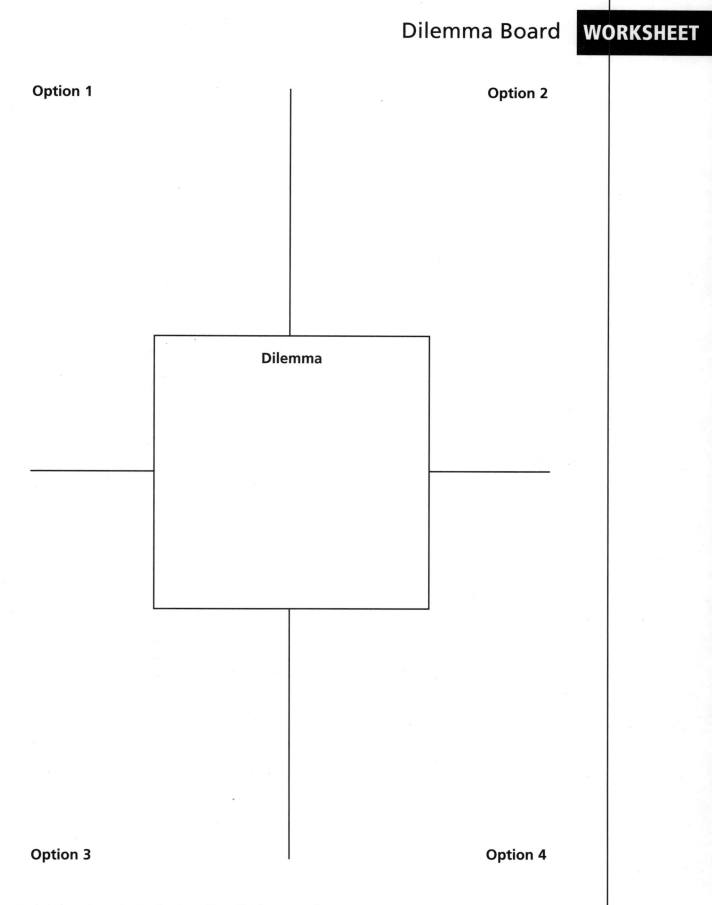

Option 1

Option 2

Dilemma

Option 3

Option 4

Discussion

14

Purpose   Although it may seem too obvious to mention, discussion deserves more attention as one of the most important and commonly used methods employed when working with groups. Its value in helping people to learn and develop can be highlighted by looking at some of its most useful applications.

Method   Small-group work and training courses do not have to be filled with trainer-led exercises. To do so would suggest that the trainer is the possessor of all knowledge whose sole purpose is to impart it to the participants. While the trainer may be an expert on the theory and technicalities of the subject, it is the participants who, usually, are the "experts" on the setting or context in which such knowledge and skills are to be applied.

The value of discussion—between pairs, in small groups or as part of a plenary session—is that it engages the participants in the learning process. Their contributions derive from their experience, ideas, thoughts and feelings. By contributing to the discussion, participants are either relating and applying the material to their own situation, or questioning and disagreeing with it because they do not see the connection to their experience. Either way, discussion is an important way for participants to test, refine, and ultimately own the course material.

Group discussion can take one of two forms—**structured** or **unstructured**.

- In **structured** discussion, the trainer will establish the initial theme, question or subject for the group to discuss. He will then listen to the discussion and endeavor to keep it on the subject by reminding participants of the original topic if it diverges too far. Structured discussion is most often used in training events and problem-solving sessions.

- In **unstructured** discussion, the opening topic may be only loosely defined, and the trainer will not make any attempt to control the direction of the conversation. Unstructured discussion is more common among mutual-support groups and other groups without formal leaders.

The art of using discussion techniques is to establish a conversation or debate within the group that does not require all comments to be directed at, or through, the trainer. Having initiated the discussion, the trainer needs to withdraw from participating in it, and will merely play a role in maintaining it when it gets stuck.

Inexperienced, newly formed or unconfident groups will tend to direct their comments to the trainer. There are several ways to avoid this, as noted below.

- Define the topic and ask participants to discuss it in smaller groups, so it is physically impossible for the trainer to be present in all the groups.

- Turn the question and comments back to the group with such remarks as:

  "Your view is more important than mine."

  "Does anyone else in the group have an answer to that?"

  "As you are the person who is likely to have to do it, what do *you* feel?"

- Give the group the task of recording their views on a flipchart sheet so attention is diverted to the sheet rather than the trainer (perhaps ask the group to nominate a spokesperson to report back).

- Give roles to people in the group to speak from during the discussion, such as "argue in favor," "argue against," "express anxiety and uncertainty."

A short discussion period serves a number of other purposes. As well as helping participants apply insights and learning from the group or course, it also encourages reflection. This is a broadening process in which each participant has the opportunity to think laterally and creatively about other aspects that might be related to the topic. Through reflection, a perspective on the learning is gained which places that learning within the network of other knowledge and skills already held by the participants.

Providing a short discussion period in pairs or small groups also offers the group leader "breathing space" in the event. This can be valuable time for the leader to reflect on how matters are going, to think about what should happen next and to prepare for contingencies.

Suitability   As suggested in Chapter 2, discussion techniques provide one of the common methods of "working with the opposite." This makes them particularly appropriate after a lengthy demonstration by the trainer or another exercise in which there has been little opportunity for participation. A discussion can usefully follow any theoretical or presentational session, and can enable group members to apply what they have just heard to their own setting.

Drawing

15

Purpose
Drawing techniques engage the creative and imaginative elements of the brain rather than the intellectual, rational and logical elements that verbal techniques tend to rely upon. They can be very helpful for illustrating feelings, emotions, perceptions and attitudes. A picture or graphic can sum up what words alone may fail to convey. Nonverbal techniques play an important part in many group activities, and drawing is a particularly simple technique that requires little preparation. If the group is too inhibited to use drawing methods, some of the same results can be obtained using cut-up magazines and pictures as a montage.

Participant risk factor **4**

Method
Drawing techniques require no more than pencil and paper. To add interest or size, the trainer or group leader may choose to use flipchart sheets and colored markers. Individuals, small groups, or the entire group can be asked to draw their view of the topic under consideration. Suggest occasionally that the drawings be completed without speaking so the emphasis is placed upon the illustration, not the explanation.

When drawings are complete, there should be plenty of time to place them on display and to discuss each one in turn. This is the time for participants to ask questions about each other's drawings, and if necessary, to offer explanations or interpretations about the way something has been shown.

The process of drawing will frequently reveal differences in ways of looking at a situation. These differences can be profitably explored by the group in considering what to do next with regard to the issue under discussion.

Examples of the technique
Here are several examples of creative drawing techniques in use:

- During a team-building session, each member is asked individually to draw the team at work, showing their view of the current relations among members.

- In another team-building session, all members of the team are asked to work together and in silence on a single large picture showing how the team works. Each person is allowed to add to the drawing made by another, but nothing may be removed. This exercise provides two sources of information: the drawing itself and the process among the team members for achieving the joint drawing.

- During a counseling session, the person receiving the counseling is asked to draw members of his or her family and their relationship one to another.

Drawing. . .

- In a planning session for an organization, staff members are asked to prepare two drawings, one representing "The way we are now" and the other showing "The way I would like us to be in a year's time." The difference between the two drawings shows the work that is required in the next 12 months; the "future" drawings of group members show the work agenda.

Possible variations

Preparing a series of drawings can be useful in incident analysis—see **Cartoons** (page 33).

Maintaining a sequence of drawings completed by members of the same group over a period of time demonstrates the history and progress of the group in a graphical way.

In some situations, more structured drawing may be appropriate. Using outline templates, participants in a personal development group can be asked to fill in a family crest to show aspects of themselves, or to complete the details of a stylized office to show their preferred working environment.

Groups that are unwilling to draw can be encouraged to make montages from pictures in newspapers, magazines and other printed photographs and materials. By cutting and pasting such prepared materials, a group can prepare a picture that illustrates a theme or topic.

Suitability

Drawing techniques are particularly useful for eliciting information about emotive or subjective topics. In the training and group-work fields, such topics concern team building, personal relationships, family histories, and personal aspirations.

Drawings are simple and require little preparation. However, because of their association with childhood, you may need to explain their benefit in an adult context and demonstrate enthusiasm for using them.

Energizers

16

Purpose   As their name suggests, energizers are activities designed to wake up and energize a group. Often short and active, energizers can be used in the early stages of a group to get people involved, or at a later stage when interest and attention are waning.

Method   An energizer can consist of any activity that reengages participants and actively reinvolves them with the group and its purpose. Many energizers rely upon physical activities for this, but choose the energizer carefully if people with disabilities are members of the group. The energizer should not exclude any participant.

The idea behind energizers is based upon the **Working with Opposites** principle discussed in Chapter 2. If a group is flagging, its members are likely to be increasingly lethargic or disengaged. An energizer uses an active alternative to change the pattern. A selection of energizers follows.

- Invite people to stand up, take three deep breaths and change seats. This is simple and quick, and gives people a new "view" of the group.

- Participants sit in a circle. One person standing in the middle invites all those with a particular attribute or characteristic to change chairs. As people move, the person in the middle attempts to sit in a vacated chair, leaving another person without a chair in the middle who repeats the process. Examples of attributes or characteristics to use could be: all those wearing gray socks; all those who ate breakfast that day; all married people; all those who have been to the Grand Canyon on vacation. The results can be entertaining and silly.

- Take a five-minute coffee break!

- Divide participants into groups of four. Ask each group to build the tallest tower possible using items found in the room. The dimensions of the items used must not exceed 9 inches in any direction. The group with the tallest free-standing structure after 5 minutes wins.

- *Fizz-Buzz*. Group members sit in a circle. The leader explains that the activity involves counting upwards from "one" around the group, with each person saying the next number. Each time a seven, a number containing seven (for example 27, 71) or a multiple of seven (14, 21, 28, and so on) is encountered, the person whose turn it is must say "Fizz" instead. The next person continues with the following number. (It's harder than you think to keep track.) Each time someone gets it wrong, the game restarts at one. When the group has the hang of this, try introducing the rule whereby all fours, numbers containing a four, and all multiples of four are replaced by the word "Buzz". The exercise usually collapses quickly in mathematical disarray. For the perfectionists, note that numbers such as 28 are "Fizz-Buzz" and 40 is "Buzz-Buzz".

- An energizer to be used during a group engaged in writing activities is to suggest that for the next 3 minutes everything must be written with the pen held in the other hand, or in backwards writing (capable of being read in a mirror).

- Try one or more of the **Trust Games** described on page 151.

- Invite participants to do simple but physically almost-impossible tasks, such as patting their heads while rubbing their chests in a circular motion; drawing on a flipchart while looking in the opposite direction; standing on one leg while holding a conversation with a partner.

- Head-game energizers involve mental rather than physical activity. Several such energizers can be based around plays on words. For example, ask a group how many words they can make using the letters of the word "management" that are relevant to the subject of management. Substitute other words as appropriate. Another variation is to ask groups to create a sentence relevant to the subject of management using successive words beginning with the letters M, A, N, A, G, E, M, E, N, T.

- For the more adventurous, this example offers a physical challenge. Participants work in pairs. The leader names two parts of the body that the pair partners have to attempt to join, such as a certain part of the first person to a certain part of the second person and vice versa at the same time. Examples are: knees to elbows; hands to feet; backsides to toes. You can be as risqué as the group is willing!

Many energizers are based on simple party games, so feel free to invent or adapt your own. The key to their success is to introduce them with enthusiasm and confidence so that any initial resistance by participants is quickly overcome.

Energizers. . .

Possible variations
Trainers may want to use energizers that are relevant to the theme of the group. For example, one trainer conducting a course on leadership skills began by asking participants to think individually of famous leaders who possessed qualities they admired. Each person had to mime that leader to a partner, who had to guess who it was. This energizer ended with a round in which each person explained his choice of leader.

Suitability
Energizers are great fun. However, the more tired and lackluster the group, the more difficult it is to persuade people to engage in energizers. They require enthusiasm and commitment from the leader. Many energizers involve a certain amount of silliness or exposure, so the leader should be prepared to take part or demonstrate what is required, to set an example and encourage others to take part. If the energizer is failing, abandon it with good grace and restore a more conventional program.

Games

17

Purpose   Games are traditionally regarded as belonging to childhood. They involve fun, discovery, entertainment and sometimes competition. However, these same elements, when employed in a training or group learning context, add interest and vitality to the process. The deliberate use of games in any group can greatly enhance learning, provided the games are selected with care to be relevant to the subject and are introduced in a way that emphasizes their seriousness and value.

Method   A huge variety of games is available for use by groups, ranging from the commercially produced ones that involve players in the use of their skill, knowledge and judgment, often in a competitive environment, to the more casual and opportunistic games requiring little preparation that are used almost on the spur of the moment to help a group overcome an impasse of some kind. It may be helpful to distinguish between informal and formal games.

Informal Games

These comprise entertaining activities that involve some or all of the group in "playing" together in a constructive way. Common ones include:

• Name games

Activities for helping group members remember each other's names include: doing a round in which each person says her name and repeats the name of everyone who has already introduced themselves; linking names to common characteristics, so each name is associated with an image; and arranging for simple interviews between participants, followed by an introduction of each person to the whole group by their interviewer.

• Trust games

Designed to establish greater trust and confidence among members of a group, trust games involve simple physical activity in which one person is dependent on others. Examples include: leading a blindfolded partner around the room; someone standing with his eyes closed in a supporting circle of colleagues and falling from side to side; and more risky games such as lying supine on the floor and being lifted into the air by eight colleagues. For more information, see Trust Games (page 151).

• Energizers

When the energy level in a group is flagging, or when a change of pace is required to reinvigorate a group, an energizing game may be appropriate. These usually involve participants in moving about, swapping chairs, or engaging in fairly frantic activity. For specific examples, see Energizers (page 63).

Informal games work if they are introduced with enthusiasm by the leader, who is able to show their relevance to the present stage of development in the group and overcome inhibitions among participants about "making a fool of themselves". Normally, this requires the leader to be an active player in the game and to set an example by initiating some of the activities. If such games are introduced apologetically or without confidence, they are more likely to meet with resistance and to fizzle out.

Formal Games

In recent years, structured games have been invented for use with groups working on particular issues. Many of these games are commercially produced with high-quality accessories and complete instructions. While some of them are competitive in nature, encouraging teams or individuals to play against each other to win, several games designed to raise awareness of issues have adopted a noncompetitive format. These are some examples:

• Business games

Lots of games have been produced to simulate different sorts of business environments. Typically they involve groups of players running different "companies" and competing with each other to gain market share and make a profit.

• Awareness-raising games

Several games invite players to learn about such sensitive topics as sex education or equal-opportunity concepts. They avoid a competitive format to encourage players to acquire knowledge and awareness in a relaxed manner. Such games often involve players throwing a die to move around a board, on which squares are marked with different instructions. These refer the player to decks of cards containing factual questions or opinion-provoking statements, to which the player responds. The object of the game is to stimulate discussion among players using the cards as prompts. The leader has some control over the game by deciding in advance which cards to select for inclusion in the game each time it is played.

• Computer games

As well as computer games of the arcade type, many computer programmers are now devising self-study and interactive games that prompt discovery and learning among users. While many of these are more suitable for individuals than groups, an increasing number can be shared among several players. They have the advantage that each player is able to progress at his own pace.

• Team games

Some games provide artificial exercises to encourage team development. Usually these establish a common task that all players must complete together and that requires their cooperation. The debriefing of the game provides an opportunity for discussing the effectiveness of this team collaboration.

Possible variations
Most games are capable of considerable variation to suit different circumstances. Sometimes a game does not need to be played through to the end to be useful as an educational tool. Other games can be adapted—by a simple change in the rules or structure—to suit a different purpose.

Suitability
Games can provide a stimulating and entertaining way to approach a subject with adults as well as young people. Often because their approach is different, games will be remembered longer than other forms of learning. While games provide a useful introduction to a subject, remember that the game is not an end in itself. It requires debriefing and discussion to consider the game's relevance and the applicability of its lessons within the wider context of the group's learning.

Handouts

18

Purpose Handouts comprise any form of written material or sample that is distributed to the participants of a course or group. The handout usually is intended to reinforce or illustrate what has been presented by the trainer. It may also act as a summary or contain a series of instructions for what the participants are expected to do next.

Method Preparing good handouts that support the work and presentations of the trainer is something of an art form. The notes provided on the Handout on page 73 are designed as a summary of the key points and as an illustration of handout methods.

Examples of the technique

- In giving a presentation on a complex subject that refers to background research and data, the speaker uses handouts to summarize the main conclusions and provide references to the research sources so listeners can follow up if they are interested.

- Before introducing an exercise that involves participants working in small groups on a series of tasks, the trainer explains the process and issues handouts to remind people what they have to do.

- Before starting a new group, the leader prepares and distributes to interested members a short handout to explain the aims of the group and the likely methods; this helps people choose whether to join.

- To support a presentation about new products to a staff group, the speaker distributes samples of the products to familiarize them with their use.

- To leave participants with a clear message at the end of a course, the group leader distributes a handout chart showing the course content in diagrammatic form, to aid its retention in participants' memory.

Possible variations Some trainers like to convert handouts into overhead transparencies for use on a projector (OHP). This is a good idea for focusing the attention of the group but, to be effective, the OHP transparency needs to be simple and clear. An accompanying handout can convey details more elaborately.

Handouts. . .

Here are some guidelines for preparing OHP transparencies:

- Use large, bold lettering throughout.

- No more than seven lines of text.

- Maintain a good-sized margin and use only a few words on each line.

- Make the transparency tall (portrait shape) rather than long (landscape shape) so it fits better on the projector.

- Use color wherever possible to generate impact.

Suitability Handouts are generally welcomed as a tangible reminder and summary of the content of any group or course. The use, design and wording of handouts should reflect the anticipated reading level of the audience.

Handout About Handouts

Each handout should have a clear purpose relating to the content of the material that directly precedes it in the work of the group. This handout summarizes the key features of a clear handout.

Handouts may be used:

- to summarize the key points of a presentation so people do not have to take their own notes;

- to convey instructions for an exercise that is to follow;

- to provide supplementary information not contained in the main presentation; and

- to provide illustrations and examples of materials discussed in the main presentation.

Prepare each handout on a separate sheet of paper with clear headings, structure and layout. Where a series of related handouts is prepared, try to employ similar styles and to number each one consecutively. The following points will help you prepare useful handouts.

- Avoid lengthy handouts and too much detail; they reduce the chance of the material being read or used.

- Avoid unnecessary jargon or abbreviations that confuse the less-experienced reader.

- Use pictures, charts and diagrams to convey ideas wherever possible.

- Use larger print sizes and good spacing of text to aid reading.

- In presentations, tell people in advance that a handout will be issued so they concentrate on listening, not taking notes.

Homework

19

Purpose

While homework is usually associated with schools, the notion of asking participants to prepare work in advance of a session or do follow-up work afterwards is a positive way of extending the effect of that session. Because the work is done away from the group, the term "homework" is adopted to describe this exercise.

Method

Any form of homework involves establishing tasks for participants to undertake outside the group sessions. There are three opportunities for this with slightly different purposes:

• **Advance homework.** Participants are asked to prepare material before the group meets. This helps focus attention on the forthcoming work and starts to engage the group members before they actually arrive. It may also check the commitment and motivation of each participant and help participants understand the nature of the work that is about to be done.

• **Mid-event homework** occurs during longer courses at a break between sessions. To maintain focus on the sessions or to complete tasks for which there is insufficient time during the sessions themselves, the trainer may assign some homework tasks to bring back to the next session.

• **Follow-up homework** refers to any work or task that participants are expected to complete after the sessions are over. While there is no check on whether this is completed, the purpose normally would be to help participants use the material from the sessions in their work and to monitor its effectiveness.

To avoid the impression of a school regime, explain that any homework is entirely voluntary and purely for the participant's own benefit — it is rare for this work to be collected and assessed. Where homework covers ground that is not otherwise contained in the main group or course, it should be regarded as an option and not something on which the main event is dependent for completion.

Homework. . .

Examples of the technique

- Distribute a self-assessment checklist to participants before a course so they can assess their existing areas of knowledge and skill.
- Ask participants to complete a diary each evening during a five-day course, containing their reflections, reactions and learning.
- Provide participants with a monitoring sheet after an event so they can determine the extent to which they apply skills learned during the group sessions.

Suitability

Homework sheets usually involve some form of written work. Participants should feel comfortable with this style of work and need to know what, if anything, will happen to their homework. Because you will not be available when the homework is completed, make the instructions clear and explicit.

Icebreakers

20

Purpose

When groups get together for the first time, participants often do not know each other well or at all. Before working together on any task, members need to go through a process of building some sort of initial relationship. Methods for doing this have been devised that are known as *icebreakers,* for the very reason that they are designed to "break the ice" between strangers.

Method

Icebreakers tend to be artificial by nature. They are ways of encouraging people to meet and talk when, under other conditions, this may not occur naturally. Some group icebreaker exercises can be complex and involved but this almost defeats their purpose: So much time and energy is spent in explaining the procedure that the exercise becomes a task in its own right. Icebreakers should be a quick and comfortable way for new participants to meet each other. The simpler and more natural the approach, the more likely it is to succeed. The ideas below range from the obvious to the more structured.

Welcoming Committee

Much of the tension can be removed from the initial meeting of any group or course if the leader or trainer is well prepared in advance. This means not only having the program materials well organized and the room laid out, but being on hand near the entrance to greet people as they arrive. A friendly word and acknowledgment goes a long way in putting people at ease. The leader can also introduce strangers to each other in much the same way as you might at a party.

The Cup of Coffee

Providing refreshments at the outset of any meeting provides its own focus. People gravitate towards the kitchen area, help each other, and ask questions ("Do you take cream?"); this leads them on to other conversations.

Getting-to-know-you Exercises

A more artificial exercise is to deliberately create time for participants to meet and talk to one or two other people—preferably people they do not already know. At its simplest, a getting-to-know-you activity involves participants forming into pairs and being given 5 minutes to talk to each other about anything. Customarily, people will ask "safe" questions about names, jobs, workplaces, distances traveled to the event, and so on.

A variation is to prepare a short list of questions on a handout, which each person asks his partner. For example: *What do you like about your present job? Why did you choose to join this group? What do you enjoy doing in your leisure time?*

After a set time, pairs end and each participant is asked to form another pair with a different person. The conversations are repeated with the same or different questions. Pairs can be re-formed three or four times.

Instead of using pairs, you can use trios, with one person answering questions from the other two. Or pairs can be asked to combine into quartets, and then quartets into octets.

At the end of the exercise, the trainer can organize feedback with the whole group in the form of a discussion round, or by each person introducing himself, or by each person being introduced by his interviewers.

Name Games

An embarrassment for many people joining a group is their difficulty in remembering the names of other participants. Several icebreaker exercises address this problem.

- Sitting in a circle, the first person says his name. The second person says his name and, pointing to the first person, adds, "And this is. . . ." The third person says his name and, pointing back to each person who has already spoken, says, "And this is. . . and that is. . . ." The exercise continues in a cumulative way until everyone is introduced and repeats the names of all the others.

- People can fail to remember names unless they have a simple "hook" to help the recall. This next exercise provides the hook. Each person draws a simple picture or sketch that represents his name. They then introduce themselves to the group and explain the picture. The association of person and picture in other participants' minds will normally help them recall the name. In a similar way, asking each person to introduce himself and add a funny or surprising personal anecdote will also help to fix names and characters in the minds of the rest of the group.

- Give each person a name tag to wear at the first session or two. Rather than typing name tags in advance—which often are too small to read, and by nature impersonal—distribute blank labels and a marker pen and invite people to write their chosen name (the one they want other people in the group to use) in large letters visible from across the room. Name tags help people memorize the names of new acquaintances.

- Posting a large sheet on the wall in clear view of everyone, with names written on the sheet in relation to where each person is sitting in the room, helps participants remind themselves of names without embarrassment.
- For young children, standing in a circle when everyone has said their name is followed by a ball game. One person throws a ball to another, saying as he does so, "My name is. . . , and I'm throwing the ball to. . . ." As the ball is thrown among players, names are reinforced by the repetition.

Tea Party

This classic and noisy icebreaker derives from the Mad Hatter's tea party in Lewis Carroll's *Alice in Wonderland*. The group forms into pairs with partners sitting facing each other in two lines down the length of the room. Each person has a quick conversation with the partner opposite for a minute. The subject of the conversation is chosen by the trainer either from a prepared list or on the spot (such as: my favorite time of year; why I have come today; what I would be doing if I were not here; why I like/hate my work; my last vacation; my ambition). At the end of the minute allowed, the trainer calls for "all change": everyone stands up and moves one chair to the left; those on the end of the line move to the front. When everyone has a new partner, the trainer announces the next topic. Every minute, "all change" is called and the exercise repeated until people have met each other or there is a natural end. The exercise is noisy because everyone is talking at once. There is an eagerness to speak because the time on each topic is short. The fun derives from the unpredictability of the topic and the rapid changes.

Possible variations   For icebreakers engaging participants in physical activities, see **Trust Games** (page 151).

Suitability   Icebreakers will work with all groups, provided a suitable selection is made of the most appropriate exercise for each group. Some sort of introduction exercise is almost always required when groups come together for the first time. When making a choice of exercise, consider the previous experience of participants, their likely willingness or resistance to participating, the amount of time available and your own enthusiasm for encouraging others to participate.

Lectures and Formal Presentations

21

Purpose Lecturing — speaking to an audience from the front of the room—is a long-established method of teaching and demonstrating. It is particularly useful when conveying information or giving an explanation that many people need to hear. In work with groups, it has tended to be discarded as an inappropriate method of engaging people's attention and working with them. However, as this section suggests, it does have a place in any repertoire of training techniques.

Method Rather than using the expression "lecturing," which gives an impression of one person addressing a large number of students, it may be more appropriate to think in terms of "giving input" to a group where one person holds the attention of all the others for a period of time. Under what circumstances might such a method be desirable? Possible situations include:

- when demonstrating how to do something, so participants can do it for themselves;

- when conveying information or instructions to a group of participants;

- when summarizing the discussion of several groups for the benefit of everyone in a plenary session; or

- when wishing to demonstrate or exercise control over all the participants together.

Because participants are not engaged directly in presentations—they are usually passive observers and listeners—it helps to make the presentation as short, focused and relevant as possible. Other ways of engaging the group's attention are to invite them to ask questions, to draw examples from their experience, and to involve them in practical aspects of any demonstration.

All inputs and presentations benefit from good forethought. There are three stages: *planning, preparation,* and the *presentation* itself.
A checklist of points to consider at each stage follows.

Planning

- Work out the overall message you wish to convey.
- Identify the key points you want others to hear — probably no more than three or four points.
- Put these points into an order that will make sense to the audience.

Preparation

- Fill in the detail around the overall message and key points.
- Work out a running order for what you want to say—try to keep it short and simple.
- Prepare whatever notes are necessary—perhaps outline notes on cards, rather than a full script.
- Prepare support materials such as slides, diagrams and other illustrations ("a picture is worth a thousand words").
- Work out a timing for the presentation so each point has sufficient time, and there is some spare time to allow for questions and interruptions.

Presentation

- If at all possible, rehearse it.
- Make sure you have all the props and equipment required.
- Organize the room to suit you and your presentation.
- Acknowledge your nervousness to the audience if necessary — it will help you relax.
- Ask the audience for feedback and questions at regular intervals; this will tell you whether they have understood.
- Be flexible; change your script to follow interesting questions and comments from the group.
- Look confident, even if you are not (by wearing favorite clothes, smiling, and so on.)

Examples of the technique

- A senior manager had responsibility for motivating his departmental managers in the implementation of a new corporate strategy. He wanted to involve these managers in deciding how the implementation should occur. At a one-day seminar, he used a 20-minute lecture presentation to outline the main aspects of the strategy. He supported this presentation with copies of the strategy report. After answering questions for another 20 minutes, he asked the departmental managers to work in small groups to consider how the strategy might affect each of their departments.

- A recently formed community group was planning to act on behalf of local residents in negotiating improvements to local housing and environmental conditions. Their own knowledge of how the local government functioned was limited, so they invited a community-relations coordinator to make a presentation to their group illustrating the role of different government departments and how they interacted.

- During a personal-development course involving outdoor activities, the participants were going to take part in a hike across some local mountains. They had trained for this activity and learned all the requisite skills. In a final briefing session, the instructor made a short presentation focusing on the key safety aspects of the expedition and reminded them of what to do if an accident occurred.

Possible variations

For more information and advice about the use of handouts and overhead projector transparencies to support your lecture or formal input, see **Handouts** (page 71).

Suitability

Presentations and lectures are often a way of controlling a group, because the attention is focused on the presenter. It is therefore a suitable technique if you want attention on the trainer or leader, rather than on participants in the group. There is also a certain danger in this: If the lecture is poor or the style fails to hold the group's attention, control is lost and there is no way of knowing how the group may react to the boredom, lack of interest or leadership vacuum that results.

Pairs

22

Purpose Working in pairs is a common technique for helping participants focus on an issue or topic and to consider its personal relevance or application. It shifts attention in the group from the trainer to the participants, who, working in pairs, can be given a wide variety of related tasks to do. The purpose of pair work is often to increase the participation of individuals in the event and to change the style of the event itself.

Method There is no single method for developing pair work. Rather, it is often a way of "going to the opposite" as described in Chapter 2. Asking participants to work in pairs on a task may serve several functions, as follows.

- During the initial stages of an event, pairing participants may introduce them to a new person, provide each person with someone else to talk to, and make them feel more comfortable.

- In pairs, participants can discuss a recent suggestion from the trainer or other source, and consider how it might apply in their situations.

- People working together as a pair can act as listeners and supports to each other's problems (see also **Triads** on page 147); this may develop into a cosupport or coworking relationship.

- Given the task of generating ideas in response to a problem or situation, two people are likely to find it more productive and creative to work as a pair, sparking ideas off each other.

- Where some people in a group have particular skills or knowledge, pairing them with others wishing to learn creates a peer-trainer relationship in which effective learning is likely to occur; this can be strengthened if each partner has something to learn from the other.

- To check how much a group has learned from a recent presentation, the trainer may ask participants to work in pairs and devise questions about it; this allows questions to be asked naturally, and allows the trainer to assess how much was assimilated.

- Moving from a plenary session to a short task carried out in pairs should succeed in "waking up" the participants and reengaging them in the event if this is necessary.

Pairs. . .

Possible variations

As indicated, pair work can be used for a variety of purposes, and is a good backup for trainers wishing to change the style or format of a group. Two particular variations are described below.

- *Peer tutoring* is the deliberate use of one pair partner to teach the other a skill within the context of a mutually supportive relationship; it is slowly being used in schools to encourage students to learn from each other as, for example, with reading. It can be used similarly with older age groups to teach clerical skills, first aid, outdoor pursuits, and a wide range of other skills.

- *Buddy relationships* describe the deliberate pairing of two people to provide mutual support for the duration of an event (which may last several sessions). During some collaborative activities, a manager and a field worker from the same social-services agency have been paired as buddies so neither can use the other as an excuse for why action may not happen.

  In work with groups of people with learning difficulties, a buddy is available to provide personal support and encouragement during the group event. For an induction course, each new member of staff may form a buddy relationship with an established staff member at a similar level so he or she can ask questions informally that might not be easy to ask of the trainer or manager.

Suitability

Pair exercises are easy to introduce and explain. They can be used regularly and at short notice in many events, or they may be planned in the program as a way of offering reflection and planning time. Often, pair exercises are combined with other techniques for a specific activity (for example, completing a drawing as a pair). Keep most pair exercises short (less than 15 minutes) so neither partner becomes bored or exhausted by the concentration that working in a pair demands.

Pencil-and-paper Worksheets

23

Purpose   Pencil-and-paper methods are often associated with school-based learning but their value should not be underestimated. Offering a task that needs to be completed on paper—either a standard page prepared as a worksheet for completion or a large flipchart sheet to be filled in—focuses everyone's attention. The techniques provide a product that is recorded on paper for others to see and read or for later reference.

Method   At the heart of most pencil-and-paper techniques lies a worksheet that participants complete, either working on their own or in small groups. The worksheet is a formatted page with prepared instructions and questions or tasks to be completed.

Worksheets can serve a wide variety of purposes:

- A questionnaire gathers data, either from participants or from people outside of the group.

- A self-assessment sheet is a particular form of questionnaire in which the person completing it rates herself against the questions asked.

- A task sheet sets out instructions to be followed in undertaking a function related to the group.

- Sentence-completion exercises provide prompts and sentence "stems" for the participant to complete in a way that is appropriate to her.

- Forms of various kinds are specifically designed to record the results of work and exercises undertaken by participants.

In preparing any worksheets for a group, irrespective of its nature, bear in mind several guidelines:

- The worksheet should explain its purpose at the beginning.

- The language and phrasing of the worksheet should be as simple as possible. Avoid jargon and acronyms wherever possible.

- By focusing on the key elements, the worksheet should be short; anything longer than two sides of a sheet 8½" x 11" tends to generate resistance.

- The use of checklists and check-boxes make it much easier to complete.

- If the worksheet requires qualitative replies to be written in, allow sufficient space for entries. Many people consider the relative length of such spaces as an indication of how much they are expected to write.

- Make clear what is going to happen to the worksheet: Is it for the person's own use? Are results to be reported to a larger group? Is it to be collected and read by someone else?

There is a critical difference between worksheets that allow participants to reflect on what they have discovered or learned about themselves or an issue, and worksheets whose structure leads to a diagnosis or "correct answer" that is revealed at the end. The former give control to the participant. The latter are sometimes criticized because they feel like a game in which the trainer subsequently produces "the truth" against which the participants' responses are being tested. This quality tends to make people feel uncomfortable.

Examples of the technique

Many examples of worksheets are provided throughout this tool kit, often to illustrate particular techniques. In this chapter, **Dilemma Boards** (page 55) and **Action Plans** (page 25) both provide examples of worksheets. Further information about specific applications is contained in the sections devoted to **Questionnaires**, **Sentence-completion Exercises**, and **Self-assessment Activities**.

Suitability

Worksheets are an excellent way of focusing the group's attention on a specific task and for ensuring that there is a definite product or outcome to any exercise. To be effective, take considerable care in the design of the worksheet so it delivers its intended objectives. Rather than regarding worksheets as simplistic in their approach, many groups welcome the clarity and directness that a well-designed worksheet can offer to their work.

Keep original copies of all worksheets in a filing system or on a computer disk for easy retrieval. Even if a worksheet is never used again in its first format, it can be the source from which an amended version is created on another occasion.

Plenaries

24

Purpose   A plenary consists of any session in which all group members form one large group to work together. This may be for the purpose of hearing a lecture from a speaker, to share results from work done in smaller working groups, or to share ideas on a common problem. What characterizes any plenary session is that the group leader has the attention of all the group members in one place.

Method   While plenary sessions may be so commonplace as to be virtually disregarded as a deliberate training technique, this underestimates their value. From the section in Chapter 2 on **Working with Opposites**, remember that one way of addressing difficulties that occur in a group is to move to the "opposite" of what is currently happening. Because much training and group work occurs in small groups, the deliberate recall of the whole group into a plenary should be a conscious, planned technique by the trainer. The use, by so many conferences and workshops, of plenary contributions from invited speakers reflects an undue reliance on one method of learning, which may be effective for the first presentation but is likely to become increasingly boring and ineffective with each subsequent platform speaker. The art of the trainer is to use plenary contributions as just one element in the whole program.

The main **benefits** of plenary sessions are that they:

- reassert the control of the trainer by focusing attention on one individual;

- enable experiences and ideas to be shared across the whole group;

- generate a sense of group identity and cohesion;

- enable common instructions and information to be given quickly and easily to all participants;

- facilitate the involvement of more reserved members by allowing them to "hide" within the larger group.

The **drawbacks** of plenary sessions are often the reverse of these advantages. They can be summarized as:

- inhibiting the participation of group members for fear of exposure to a larger group;

- diminishing the sense of control and ownership that any one participant has in the event;

- reducing the opportunities for individual members to contribute in an active way to the learning process.

Plenary sessions are most likely to be used at these particular points in the program:

- *during the introduction,* when participants need to be welcomed and given a sense of whole-group identity;
- *for lectures* designed to convey information for the benefit of the whole group;
- *during feedback sessions,* when work done by smaller groups is to be shared with the whole group;
- *at the end,* when it is important to mark the achievements of group members and signify the end of the group.

Possible variations

There is a danger of plenary sessions being dull and static because they rely upon one or two individuals to retain audience interest. Plenary sessions can be varied and made more interactive by the use of different formats, as described below.

- *Technology* such as slides, film or video will retain the attention of the audience for longer if they are interesting and relevant to the presentation.
- A *question-and-answer format,* in which the presenter responds to questions from the large group, helps enliven the presentation and makes sure it remains linked to the interests of the audience.
- A *plenary* in which different members of the group take responsibility for contributing different sections of the presentation will help link the plenary to the interests and identity of the group.

Suitability

Plenary sessions undoubtedly have their uses in most group programs but in the past this has tended to be overrated. As with all techniques, they should be used in appropriate parts of the program and form part of a much wider range of styles adopted throughout the whole program.

Problem-Solving

25

Purpose

Many problem-solving exercises have been devised to promote team-work through the development of creative, supportive and innovative collaboration approaches. Modeling an artificial example of problem solving helps groups transfer the same skills and cooperation to their real work together.

Method

Numerous problem-solving activities have been created by different trainers; it is only possible here to outline a few of the different approaches.

Building Tasks

Group members are given the task of building a structure using particular materials in a set time. The leader needs to prepare a selection of materials in advance. In an indoor site, these may include building blocks, small solid objects, rubber bands, poles, cardboard, paper clips. The task may be to build a structure that represents something relevant to the event (such as your team, your workplace, the future) or the task may simply be to build the tallest structure. In each case, give a time limit for the exercise. On an outdoor site, building tasks have involved many different problems: getting an object from A to B over a series of obstacles, building a bridge over a stream, building a floating raft, erecting a tower. Make sure suitable materials are available and that appropriate safety instructions are given.

Simulations

An artificial simulation — such as the production of a news program on video, as described in the section on **Simulations** (page 131)—is an excellent way of generating a dynamic problem requiring a creative solution and teamwork.

Real Problems

Some groups are at a stage of development where they are ready to apply their skills and knowledge to tackle real problems they face, with the group leader acting as a facilitator to the process. In this case, the group should agree on the definition of the problem and use a variety of techniques such as **Brainstorming** (page 31), **Critical-incident Analysis** (page 47), **Case Studies** (page 43), **Small Groups**(page 147) and **Role-play** (page 103), to solve it.

All problem-solving activities should be adequately debriefed through discussion involving all participants at the end. The debriefing should focus not just on what happened but on *why* it happened in the way that it did, the relationships and processes among people, and the learning points for future problem solving.

Suitability   Problem-solving techniques can be great fun, particularly if they are artificial in nature but clearly relevant to the purpose of the group. Where the task relates to a real problem faced by the group, trust and commitment need to be established among group members first before the problem has a real chance of being solved.

Psychodrama

26

Purpose

Drama techniques are commonly used with groups in **Role-play** (page 103) and **Simulations** (page 131) to recreate or rehearse situations members encounter. These techniques have many applications, which are discussed in those sections. Psychodrama methods involve a particular form of role-play that integrates aspects of psychology into the dramatic presentation. Whereas role-play is most commonly used to rehearse actions, psychodrama methods are more inward-looking. They are designed to help participants gain an insight into their own thought processes and personal decision-making. While it uses the medium of a group to facilitate this learning, the technique usually focuses on the situation faced by one individual within the group. This situation is explored through psychodrama using other group members to represent aspects of the difficulty.

Method

Psychodrama methods draw upon a wide body of creative work, including gestalt counseling, psychotherapy and other modeling techniques. In the context of training and group work it is inappropriate to explain the detail of each of these skills here. In a therapeutic context, these skills need considerable understanding and rehearsal to be used effectively. In the hands of an inexperienced practitioner, they may not help or even damage individual participants. The trainer who wishes to learn more about the methods is advised to get specialist training. The discussion here is restricted to a description of how simple psychodrama methods can be integrated into role-plays to enhance their potential and diversify their use. In doing so, the intention is to foster a more creative use of role-play — one in which the trainer is encouraged to experiment with different sorts of roles and varied applications. Each of the examples that follows illustrates how aspects of a psychodrama approach can be incorporated into a standard role-play.

Examples of the technique

Conflicting Pressures

A group member is exploring a personal situation in which various pressures are being exerted on him and each is pushing in a different direction. The trainer works with him individually to clarify the central problem and the way in which each pressure is experienced. The rest of the group listens to the explanation without comment.

The trainer asks the individual whether he would like to explore the effect of these pressures in a more tangible way. Each pressure source is given a simple name. Volunteers from the rest of the group are invited to play the "voice" of each of these pressures, and each character takes a seated position around the individual.

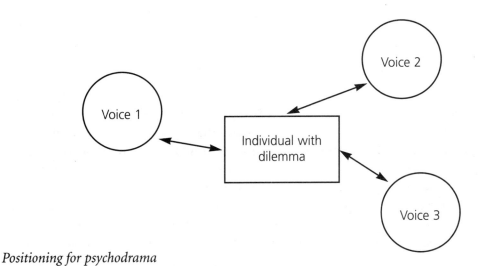

Positioning for psychodrama

The trainer tells the individual that he can ask questions of each character, who responds in a manner consistent with that particular pressure. The individual can turn to different voices at any time. Voices only speak directly to the individual, not to each other. They are "switched on" and "switched off" by the central individual. In this way, the individual builds a dialog among the voices that illustrates his central dilemma. He can ask voices to respond to comments made by others and to come up with further pressures.

The ability of each voice to sustain a particular pressure or emphasis will depend on briefing the group. Those playing the roles sometimes fear they will not be able to sustain the role in the manner expected by the individual. Yet experience shows that most voices are quickly able to invent replies and comments that are consistent with their chosen role. Because they have to invent new material, they often lead the individual into new arguments.

The individual, with the support of the trainer, has to have control over when the role-play ends. In the debriefing of the individual afterwards, the emphasis is not upon how well each character played the voice but on what insights the individual gained into the decision he faces.

Human Statues

This form of psychodrama has been derived from family therapy methods and often is used as a team-building technique.

The object of the activity is to depict the relationships among individual group members in a visual way. One volunteer from the group is invited to be the sculptor. She is invited to create a tableau of the current state of relations among people in the group by placing them physically in relation to one another around the room. Some may kneel, others stand

and so on. Each statue may be given a facial expression by the sculptor. Group members should comply with instructions from the sculptor and not speak during the process of being placed as statues. The tableau can be made dynamic by showing changes in the relationships among the statues at different times in the life of the group. Other members can be invited to act as the sculptor to show their different perceptions. Clearly, each sculpture requires considerable time for debriefing afterwards.

Further guidance on using methods is given in the section on **Sculpting** (page 117).

The Role-play Debate

This technique uses role-play as a method to help a group explore a series of options or alternatives—perhaps before reaching an important decision. The group defines the issue and identifies the main options or alternatives from among which it wishes to choose. To illustrate, the group may identify three options, such as "For", "Against" and "Status Quo". Three players volunteer to act each of these three roles in the role-play. They sit in the middle, facing each other. Each player can only speak to the others from his role perspective; that is, arguing solely in favor of, say, the "Status Quo", and in opposition to the arguments made by "For" and "Against".

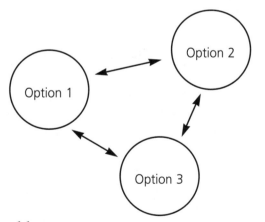

Positioning for role-play debate

One player begins by explaining her argument. The others respond from their role perspective. In role, players can challenge each other, make counter arguments and attempt to demolish the arguments of the other two. In this way, the whole group is helped to understand the issues involved in choosing from among the three courses of action by having each defined so clearly. While some players may need support in sustaining their role, this technique usually develops a momentum in which players quickly find arguments to defend themselves and attack others. The role-play should be stopped when the issues have been explored and the group is ready to make a decision.

Solo Role-plays

It is possible to use psychodrama techniques in some situations in which there is only one player, by drawing on models developed in gestalt approaches to counseling. Here the facilitator works with one individual who expresses a conflict or dilemma that may be usefully explored using role-play methods. With only one player, the individual has to play all the roles, with the guidance of the facilitator. Working together, the individual and the facilitator discuss the problem situation and identify the main options. Each role is represented by a different chair or cushion arranged in a semi-circle.

Positioning for solo role-plays

The facilitator asks the individual to sit on one chair and to speak or act from that role. When appropriate, the facilitator directs the individual to move to another chair and respond from that role. By moving among the chairs, the individual assumes each of the different roles and "answers himself." He can have arguments with himself in another role. In the debriefing session afterwards, the facilitator must help the individual decide which role (or feeling, or decision) felt most comfortable, and why. This is a use of role-play as part of counseling and all considerations relating to the nondirective use of counseling should be kept in mind before introducing solo role-plays.

Suitability The use of psychodrama methods within role-plays requires confidence and sensitivity on the part of the trainer. They should not be used by those who lack experience in role-play methods generally. Such techniques require a clear commitment from group members and as such are unlikely to achieve a positive result unless the group has been working together for some time and has built trust and confidence among its members. Despite these reservations, such extensions to role-play methods can be particularly effective in group and individual problem-solving sessions.

Questionnaires

Purpose
Many people are familiar with using questionnaires to gather information. When used in group work or training sessions, question- naires can provide information for use by the group and be used as a self-assessment exercise for individual members. Questionnaire surveys can be carried out either by participants with people outside the group, or with each other.

Method
Questionnaires can be devised to suit many purposes. Examples include:

- a training checklist completed by participants in the past and required in the future;
- a survey of users' views on services provided by the group;
- a structured analysis of a recent event or incident;
- a feedback sheet gathering reactions to various group proposals;
- a self-assessment list of personal skills and ratings on a subject.

Questionnaires are a pencil-and-paper technique, so they require preparation in advance of their use. Questionnaires devised on the spot tend to be limited in their effectiveness. By planning ahead, you can construct questionnaires to suit specific purposes and increase the chance of the survey sheet being completed fully and the resulting information used properly. Consider the following factors in devising a questionnaire:

Clear Purpose

People who complete questionnaires want to know why the survey is being carried out and how the results will be used. State the purpose at the top of the questionnaire in an easy-to-understand way without lengthy explanation.

Logical Layout

It is a good idea to begin any questionnaire with simple questions so the respondent is drawn into it. Examples might include data about the age or sex of the respondent. Ask factual questions before those that ask for opinions and feelings. Group together questions on the same subject and avoid duplicating questions. It is a good idea to end with a question that enables the respondent to add any other comments she thinks were not covered elsewhere.

Quantitative or Qualitative Design

Quantitative surveys collect information that can be analyzed

Questionnaires

numerically and statistically, sometimes using a computer. This is useful if you want to prove something or demonstrate the degree of support for a proposal. Quantitative surveys require questions that can be answered with simple "yes/no" responses or with a number. To make them easier to complete, check boxes and checklists are likely to figure in the design.

Qualitative surveys collect impressionistic, subjective and nonstandard responses. Respondents write their answers in a space provided on the form, usually in an unstructured way. This is useful if you want to collect opinions and new ideas. The difficulty with qualitative surveys is that they require more time to analyze, as each return has to be studied individually and aggregate "totals" of views are more difficult to show. For this reason, qualitative surveys should be used only when the survey involves a small number of respondents (say, fewer than 20).

Confidentiality

Respondents often want to know who will see the completed sheets and whether they will be identified. Asking people to add names may encourage more thoughtful responses; it may also deter people from giving frank answers if these are critical. A questionnaire used as part of a self-assessment exercise should make clear that the participant will retain control over the completed questionnaire and its interpretation.

Language

Try to avoid complex language and jargon, no matter who the intended audience is. Straightforward language, short sentences, good grammar and punctuation are understood by most people.

Overall Length

This is a difficult issue. Respondents may not complete questionnaires that appear very long. On the other hand, short questionnaires may not produce sufficient information for your purposes. Keep in mind two rules of thumb. A length of two pages (one sheet printed on both sides) is convenient; restrict the questionnaire to four sides at most. Work out your most important questions first. If there is space left, consider additional questions.

Field-testing

Very few questionnaires work well in their original form. The author is often in the weakest position to see a questionnaire's limitations. Get a second opinion on a questionnaire before you use it. Test it out with half-a-dozen people (who need not have much knowledge of its subject matter); they will point out obvious defects.

Questionnaires

Examples of the technique

- A trainer working with a local action group wanted to establish which areas of knowledge and skill group members felt confident about, and what subjects were the priority for future training. He devised a questionnaire that group members completed at the end of their first session together.

- Another trainer was running an event for 15 people, looking at techniques for handling difficult customers. To get participants thinking about the course before it began, she circulated a short questionnaire in advance. This questionnaire asked participants to think about the last two occasions when they had been faced with a difficult customer. They were asked questions about the attitude of the customer, their own attitude at the time, their attitude subsequently, and what they did during the incident. Participants were asked to bring their completed questionnaires with them to the course and to use them as the basis for case studies.

- At the end of a short course on time management, the trainer circulated a questionnaire for participants to complete and use themselves. The questionnaire listed each of the main subjects covered during the course. There were two columns to complete. In the first, participants stated what they were doing about each subject before the course, and in the second, they set out what they intended to do as a result of the course.

- An environmental campaign group wished to raise public awareness about plans for a new road. It decided to carry out two questionnaire surveys of the general public. The first asked drivers in the area about their trips to determine whether a road of the scale proposed was necessary. The second asked people whose homes and businesses would be affected by the new road for their reactions. The group prepared and published a report using quantitative statistics from the driver survey to show that only a smaller road was necessary, and qualitative comments from the second survey demonstrating the adverse environmental impact of the original proposal.

Possible variations

Questionnaires are similar in nature to other pencil-and-paper techniques for use with groups such as **Self-assessment Activities** (page 123), **Checklists** (page 39) and **Critical-incident Analysis** (page 47).

Suitability

Survey sheets and questionnaires can be used by most groups possessing literacy skills at a level demanded by the questionnaire. They are easy to complete and can generate much useful information for subsequent use by the group.

Ranking, Sorting and Prioritizing

28

Purpose
When groups generate ideas and examples, using techniques such as brainstorming or discussion, the volume of ideas is often greater than the group can handle in the time available. The suggestions are also of variable quality: some are more relevant, important or accurate than others. Having constructed such a list, the group needs a method for ranking or prioritizing the suggestions. This section offers a range of such techniques.

Methods
Group Voting

Voting is a common technique for making choices. It can be adapted in various ways for use with groups. One of the simplest, is to give participants three votes each (for example) to distribute among a list of perhaps 12 items. They have a minute to consider the list, which might be displayed on a flipchart, and decide how to allocate their three votes. The leader calls on each person in turn to announce his three choices. These are recorded by the leader with checkmarks on the flipchart against the respective items. The result is a visual representation of the priorities chosen by the group — those items collecting the most checkmarks being the highest priorities.

Auction Votes

This is a more subtle form of voting and selecting. The leader explains that the items on the flipchart list are to be "auctioned off" and that participants must make bids for their inclusion in the final selected list. Each person begins with, say, five tokens. These tokens are similar to votes and are used as currency in the exercise. As with group votes, each person is allowed a minute or two to decide how to use his tokens to "purchase" items from the list. Tokens can be used to prioritize between one and five items because each participant must decide not only which items on the list to select but also what weight to attach to each, as reflected by the number of tokens to be attached to it. For example, if someone is very eager to see one item prioritized, she may award all five tokens to it; another person may not have a strong preference and so distribute the five tokens among three, four or five items. The resulting scores demonstrate the prioritized items and the strength of feeling about each.

Card Sort

Various ranking exercises are based on the use of index cards, each containing one item from the original list of suggestions to be prioritized. In its most basic form, small groups are given a set of cards and asked to lay them out face up; they must discuss the cards and arrange them in order of importance. The arrangements from different small groups are compared.

Combined Sort

This card-sort variation requires each individual to be given a complete set of the same cards. The individual prepares his personal set of priorities based on the cards. Individuals then combine as pairs and are asked to discuss their individual priorities and agree a joint list. Pairs then combine as quartets to compare the pair sets and produce a priority list as a quartet. This process continues until one priority list is agreed on and produced by the whole group.

Diamond Ranking

This variation of a card sort is best used when the group leader has some control over the number of options, because it requires exactly nine items to be ranked or priortized. One difficulty with ranking exercises is that often people want to give two or more items the same rank placement. This distorts the notion of a straightforward priority list by producing an uneven shape. Diamond ranking recognizes that often one item is the most preferred and one the least, but that others may be bunched together—creating the list's "diamond" shape.

The group leader prepares nine items on separate cards to be prioritized or ranked. Small groups are given a set of the cards and are asked to arrange them in a diamond pattern:

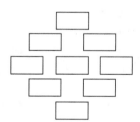

The single items at the top and bottom of the diamond are the most and least preferred; the two items below and above these are next in order; the three items across the center are of middle-order importance with little to differentiate them. You might use prepared photographs or cards that can be ranked and sorted in this manner.

Suitability   Ranking and prioritizing are almost inevitable in most groups and training courses where participants have the opportunity to generate ideas. The amount of time that can be allocated to any prioritizing technique will depend on the circumstances of each event, so you should have a repertoire of such techniques in your tool kit to help the group reach its decisions.

Role-play

29

Purpose   Role-plays are one of the most powerful techniques used with groups to assist learning. They can also be among the most complex to plan and manage in an effective way. A well-run role-play should have a strong positive impact, but a poor one is likely to result in criticism, frustration and, potentially, resentment or anger. This section provides extensive guidance for using role-plays in a constructive way. I offer suggestions for some of the many creative variations that can be developed to enhance the learning from role-plays.

Role-plays are used for various purposes. Some most common are:

- Practicing specific skills in a "pretend" situation akin to the real one
- Rehearsing actions or behaviors in a protected environment before using them in the real world
- Exploring alternative actions or behaviors to examine their consequences — again, in a protected environment
- Exploring personal attitudes or feelings to gain personal insights or to assist in personal decision-making
- Building confidence through practice or rehearsal of an event.

Method   The process of setting up and running a role-play exercise normally requires attention to a series of steps. Most of the problems trainers and participants experience in role-plays stem from one or more of these steps being inadequately completed or even omitted. The full sequence comprises:

Step 1: Planning the role-play in advance

Step 2: Preparing the script for the role-play

Step 3: Informing and engaging participants in the role-play

Step 4: Running the role-play activity

Step 5: Stopping the role-play

Step 6: Bringing participants out of role

Step 7: Debriefing the role-play

Step 8: Learning through discussion from the role-play

Step 9: Transferring the learning to the real world

Each of these steps is examined in more detail on the following pages, with suggestions for their successful completion.

Step 1: Planning the Role-play in Advance

All activities used for training or with groups deserve good planning, but this is particularly the case with role-plays because of the risks involved. The trainer needs to ask:

Why am I using a role-play exercise?

Will the activity contribute to the overall purpose of the group? Are participants likely to see its relevance? Will participants cooperate in a potentially threatening exercise? How will I introduce the role-play so it is perceived as relevant and realistic by the participants?

When should a role-play technique be used?

Experience demonstrates that participants need to feel confident and comfortable with each other before they will engage in a role-play. As a rule of thumb, role-plays are far less likely to work in the first half of any course. They require trust to be established between participants, and this only comes from deliberate trust-building exercises (see **Trust Games,** page 151) and familiarity.

How is the role-play to be controlled?

Is the script to be prepared by the trainer or the participants? The latter gives more control over the process to the participants but may take the role-play in a direction different from that intended by the trainer. Who is going to do what if the role-play goes off-course?

How much time should be allowed?

Another rule of thumb is that role-plays always take longer than anticipated. Even the simplest role-play can take 10 minutes to explain, 20 minutes to run, 20 minutes to debrief and 10 minutes to conclude. Allow at least as much time to debrief the role-play as the role-play itself takes to run. Many, many role-plays require a half-day session to organize properly. If you don't have this much time, it's probably better to use another technique. Role-plays that cannot be adequately debriefed should not be attempted.

By their nature, role-plays are unpredictable. Even with a script for the role-play prepared in advance, those involved are expected to invent dialog and actions in the activity. If the subject matter of the role-play involves people's personal feelings and behaviors, they can quickly become involved at the emotional level. Don't avoid that situation, because role-plays are often intended to engage people through their genuine responses. However, you must expect and be prepared for a range of unpredictable outcomes—and feel confident in handling them.

Step 2: Preparing the Script for the Role-play

A role-play centers on recreating an actual, anticipated or imaginary "scene". If you view this technique as a mini-play, this scene will probably involve dialogue and action. We can call this dialogue and action a *script*. Normally, plays have a complete script, but this would defeat the purpose of a role-play. The script for a role-play involves two elements:

- a clear description of the starting point; for example, what is the context, what led up to this point, who is involved, in what capacity? and

- an indication of how each person might react or behave after the role-play begins—this is often referred to as the *brief*.

In preparing the role-play, everyone must understand the starting point. If participants have agreed upon the background leading up to the situation enacted in the role-play, there will be fewer awkward interruptions for explanations. While each person needs to understand his or her point of view in the role-play, the group should avoid any detailed scripting of the part. The role-play should aim to be spontaneous within its established context. Role-plays do not have a predetermined outcome; their purpose is to explore what might happen, and how different actions or statements might influence the outcome.

Some participants—particularly those who are young or lack confidence—require some assistance in interpreting their brief and generating suitable responses, but this help should not extend as far as preparing a detailed script of what to say or do. The essence of a role-play is that it evolves and is made up as the action and events proceed.

This starting point and briefing can either be prepared in advance by the trainer or generated by the group members. Off-the-shelf role-plays presented by the trainer, may be easier to administer and introduce for the trainer, but tend to be less valuable for participants. They may refer to common situations but they are unlikely to match the direct experience (or fears) of the group. Where time permits, invite the participants to identify suitable role-play situations from their own past experience or from situations they are unsure how to handle. Be careful to distinguish the former real event from the artificial role-play: While the starting points should be the same, the role-play will evolve differently—its purpose is not to repeat the real event, but to look at what happens in similar (not identical) situations.

Step 3: Informing and Involving Participants in the Role-play

Most participants have reservations about joining role-plays. Their reservations stem from past experiences of badly handled role-plays, a reluctance to be seen "acting", lack of confidence, or an unwillingness to be "shown up" in front of peers. It is the trainer's responsibility to create a safe learning environment for every member of the group. One way of achieving this is to give as much control over the process of the role-play to the participants themselves, while making it clear that the trainer will ensure the well-being of everybody involved. The trainer can do many things to help participants become engaged in a role-play:

- Build trust among participants long before a role-play is mentioned. Help them get to know each other.

- Tell participants what is going to happen and how it will work. Keeping people informed always removes some of the mystique surrounding role-plays. Sometimes it is worth avoiding the phrase "role-play" by saying: "Let's recreate that difficult situation here in this room to examine how else it might have been handled"; or "Let's pretend we're about to meet so-and-so and then we can see what we might actually do."

- Involve the group in identifying situations from their experience to use as the starting point for the role-play to increase the relevance of the exercise.

- Negotiate the safeguards for the role-play so everyone is clear about the rules. Depending on the circumstances, these might include: no shouting, no physical touching, being able to stop the role-play when you feel uncomfortable (make sure everyone knows the stop signal), no reporting on the role-play outside the group, confidentiality. Give participants the opportunity to add and agree on their own safeguards.

- Let people choose whether to participate or not. Those that do not take part can be observers, taking notes about what happens for the debriefing later. In most cases, each of the roles should be taken by a volunteer, not allocated by the trainer. It is risky to take a central role—particularly one that involves handling a difficult situation—so participants need to be encouraged to choose this role for themselves.

- Remind people that the point of the role-play is not necessarily to "get it right" but to practice, explore or rehearse responses to a situation in the safety of the group, so they will be better equipped to handle such situations and decisions.

Step 4: Running the Role-play Activity

If the exercise has been set up well, running it should be the easiest part—although it will always be a little unpredictable. The way you run the role-play will depend on your personal style of working with groups and on the content of the role-play itself.

- **DO** be enthusiastic about the value of a role-play, so people are encouraged to participate.
- **DO** stay alert to what is happening at all times; even when it is going well, you should make notes (either mentally or on a notepad) for use in the debriefing.
- **DO** enforce whatever safeguards have been agreed to—and to protect players from any sort of harm.
- **DO** keep checking whether to stop the role-play, either because all the key points have been covered, or because it is losing direction.
- **DO** help or encourage people directly if they are struggling with their roles.
- **DON'T** try to make the action or dialogue follow some line you think is appropriate—let it follow its own course.
- **DON'T** become a player yourself, because this would give you inappropriate control and prevent your having an overview of the exercise.
- **DON'T** communicate your own apprehension about what might happen.
- **DON'T** forget why you are using a role-play in the first place.

Step 5: Stopping the Role-play

All role-plays need an ending; the difficulty lies in deciding when and how. For role-plays based upon practicing skills or rehearsing behaviors, this judgment reflects the amount of practice or rehearsal required, not whether a successful "outcome" to the role-play itself has been reached. In most situations, it is not necessary to prolong the role-play to its natural end—most of the learning is available to participants long before this point.

Lengthy role-plays also increase the anxiety of participants. Far better to have five or 10 minutes of quality role-playing than 30 minutes of an extended and mediocre exercise.

Depending on the circumstances, the trainer may decide to bring the role-play to an end, or the players can be given control. Either way, a clear signal needs to be given to everyone, both playing and observing, that the role-playing part of the exercise is now finished. If the action is stopped but could be continued, one way of checking what might happen is to do a round of all the players (see **Rounds,** page 115). The trainer asks each player in turn to say "how I am feeling at this point in my role" or "what I think would happen next" or "how I feel, in my role, this situation would eventually be resolved."

Step 6: Bringing Participants Out of Role

This is a critical step in the process of running any role-play—but often it is omitted or mishandled. No matter how involved people have been in the role-play, they must have the opportunity to leave their role behind and return to their true selves. This is particularly important when the role-play has released strong feelings or has dealt with stressful situations. Even if the role-play appears to have been straightforward, time should still be given to bringing participants out of their roles. Do this immediately after the role-play has finished and before the debriefing.

Taking people out of role enables them to distinguish between their actions or thoughts in role and those that they actually hold. Where emotions have been evoked, it should help people to leave those feelings with the role character and not continue them within the group outside the role-play. In short, this step is about helping people return to the "here and now" and to reaffirm who they really are.

Techniques for helping people come out of role sometimes seem artificial, but this does not invalidate their importance. Some common techniques for helping people include:

- asking participants to stand up, move around and sit down in a different chair
- asking people to move to a different room for the debriefing
- asking people to work in pairs (perhaps with someone who was an observer) and to talk for a few minutes about a favorite place, their plans for the evening, their family, a good film. . . anything, provided it has nothing to do with the subject of the role-play
- asking each person in turn to affirm their own name and their real job
- inviting people to write details of their allocated role and character on a piece of paper, and then symbolically crumple the piece of paper and throw it into a wastebasket in the middle of the room.

Combine two or more of these methods if required.

Step 7: Debriefing the Role-play

Running the role-play is, at most, only half the technique. Equally if not more important is the debriefing of what happened. During the debriefing, the processes that occurred during the role-play are examined and discussed. This can involve just the players or the players and the observers together. The trainer's role is to help participants gain as much insight as possible into what happened, why it happened, and what could have been done or said to change the outcome.

Depending on the nature of the role-play, the trainer might want to focus on what actions triggered what responses, what actions or skills were most effective, which behaviors did not work, and what decisions were reached.

Debriefing can be done simply by letting people talk about what they experienced during the role-play. However, with many groups, it may be preferable to have a simple structure for the debriefing session that enables everyone to contribute in a constructive way. These are some techniques to use in a debriefing session. They can be used in isolation or together.

- Invite each player in turn to say what he found happening in his role.

- Ask the observers to say what they noticed, either about the whole role-play or about one character in the exercise (you can ask at the beginning of the role-play for each observer to "track" a different player).

- Lead the session by focusing on key questions such as: What comment led to such-and-such an action happening? How might a particular outcome have been avoided? What worked well? What could be done differently next time? and so on.

- Create small groups to identify and discuss five key aspects the role-play.

- Watch a video replay of the role-play to prompt discussion of significant moments (see below).

The debriefing of a good role-play will take far longer to complete than the role-play itself. This illustrates the fact that it is often the micro-behaviors (the small gestures and comments that we make) that determine what happens, not some grand strategy. Role-play should heighten our awareness of the importance of such micro-behavioral analysis.

Before the debriefing is concluded, ask an open question about other points participants wish to raise. This gives people a final opportunity to leave their role behind, or to ask about something from the activity they do not understand.

More than almost any other technique used to help groups learn and develop, role-plays have attracted criticism and resistance. Participants often have arguments for denying what happened in the role-play or for minimizing its value. It is, of course, the trainer's responsibility to make sure the role-play runs smoothly and effectively, but there are counterpoints to make when participants show resistance to the points made in the debriefing. Rather than tackling some of these points directly, the trainer may find it more profitable to engage other participants in any discussion about the relevance and realism of the role-play, by asking, for instance: "To what extent do other people think this role-play felt like a situation you might encounter in real life?"

Some common resistances—and their counterpoints—are:

"It wasn't real because I never got into my role."

Observers will comment on how much "in role" someone was. Even if one person was not fully in role, other people may have been acting fully in role. What determines how we react either in or out of role?

"In the real world, I would have behaved differently."

Role-plays are not the real world: They are a practice or rehearsal for the real world. What would have been different? Why does this participant behave differently in practice from reality?

"But that was not how it actually went."

True — if the role-play has the same starting point as a previous real situation. But the point of the exercise is to examine what *could* have happened or *might* have happened—and why—for future use, not to recreate something exactly that is in the past.

"Role-plays are always artificial—they're not the same as the real thing."

True also; that's why they're called *role-plays*. But they are the nearest thing we have to recreating a real event and as such, there should be parallels between them that we can learn from. While it is running, a role-play is actually a real thing in its own right.

"I behave differently in role-plays than I do in the real world."

This is inevitably true to some extent. However, we do not entirely change the factors that determine our actions just because it is a role-play. One way of explaining it is to view the role-play as a *harmonic* (to borrow a musical analogy) of the real thing—the basic underlying actions and pressures are the same, even if their form is somewhat different.

Step 8: Taking the Learning from the Role-play

The debriefing may be complete in itself, or it may require an additional opportunity for each participant to consider how he can use insights gained from the exercise in his or her own work. A period of reflection can be allowed either for personal note-taking and action planning (see **Action Plans,** page 26) or for pairs to support each other in thinking about possible applications of the role-play material in their own work.

Step 9: Transferring the Learning to the Real World

The test of any role-play is whether participants can carry the skills or behavior rehearsed or the decisions reached during the role-play into the real world. This is the *learning transference.* Preparation for this transfer may occur through reflective time and action planning. Depending on the circumstances, the trainer may wish to arrange a time when participants can meet again to discuss how lessons from the role-play were used in practice.

Example of a role-play technique in action

This is a simple example of the process for running a role-play, using many of the points discussed above.

Preparing the Scene

The trainer and group are working together on the problems of communicating with difficult clients. Considerable trust has been established among group members by sharing their professional experiences in this area, and through joint work on other, less-threatening exercises. The trainer judges that the time has arrived for practicing actual communications skills in a series of role-plays.

Having introduced the idea, the group brainstorms a half-dozen examples of situations that have arisen (or might arise) in which a staff member has to deal with a difficult client. The background to each is sketched and recorded briefly. The group selects three of these examples to pursue in more detail through short role-plays.

Before asking for volunteers, the trainer sets out a series of safeguards for the exercise. These include: Client behaviors are to be difficult but not impossible; role-plays are to last no more than eight minutes; confidentiality of real cases is to be respected; and no physical assaults by clients on staff is allowed in the role-plays. These are discussed and agreed.

The trainer asks for volunteers to act as clients and staff members. It is not necessary for the person who suggested each scenario to take part, either as a client or staff member, but he may have "first refusal" of any role. Roles are allocated. Nonplayers are asked to observe the staff members and make notes on effective and ineffective interventions during the role-plays.

Small groups spend a few minutes devising more detail about the background for each role-play and establishing a starting point that is explained to the respective players.

The Role-play in Action

The first role-play begins. The trainer remains in the background but is alert and watchful. After six minutes, the trainer decides that the role-play situation has reached stalemate and ends the action. Both players are asked to give a quick comment about how they feel at that point. They then pair up with a nonplayer who takes them out of role.

Meanwhile, the second role-play begins. This time, the staff member is more successful in communicating with the client and the role-play runs the full eight minutes before it is stopped. The process of bringing players out of role is repeated as the third and final mini-role-play is set up. This time, communication between the two players quickly descends into mud-slinging, which goes nowhere. In order to maintain the ground rules, the trainer intervenes to stop the action, and both players are helped to move out of their roles.

Debriefing the Role-plays

Now the group has three short role-plays to examine. The trainer begins by asking the participants who played staff members to say how they felt each scene went, and to highlight their own assessment of their strengths and weaknesses. Next, the trainer asks the observers to comment on the people they were each watching. Finally, the conversation is opened to those clients with roles to comment on what did and did not work.

This leads to a general discussion about communication techniques that work and to alternative ways in which these particular situations might have been handled. After 40 minutes, the conversation is still going strong.

Transferring to the Real World

For the final 10 minutes of the exercise, the trainer asks each person to work with a partner and to highlight the three most significant points each has learned from participating or watching these role-plays about handling difficult or awkward clients. These points are written down for participants to take away and use later.

Possible variations

The variety of ways in which role-play techniques can be used or extended is considerable. Trainers and group leaders have devised a huge range of different approaches and devices for use in various circumstances. This section gives a few suggestions for:

- additional techniques to use in running a role-play; and
- other forms of role-plays.

Additional Techniques to Use in Running a Role-play

Described below are some devices I have found useful in getting the most from a role-play exercise. Consider using them if they are likely to help in your own circumstances.

- **Cartooning**

  One way of generating an outline script for a role-play is to use cartooning methods (see **Cartoons,** page 33). This enables participants to sketch out the sequence of events leading up to and into the role-play. It provides a framework of ideas for the action and dialogue that occurs in the role-play. Cartooning is particularly useful with less-confident groups because it helps them devise the script; but beware of losing the spontaneity and unpredictability of the role-play.

- **Tagging**

   Many role-plays require one volunteer to take on a difficult role such as authority figure, counselor, problem-solver: the person who is expected to manage and change the situation presented by the role-play. This is an exposed role, because the volunteer's own skills and abilities are on the line for colleagues in the group to see and appraise. For this reason, such roles are often hardest to fill when looking for volunteer players. A way of supporting such exposed players is to set up a tagging arrangement. Two people volunteer to share one difficult role. One person at a time is involved in the role-play while the partner remains at a short distance from the group. When the first person gets stuck in the role, or recognizes that she needs a break, the partner takes over as a "tag" and continues the role-play from the same point. In effect, they swap places. This is not as confusing at it seems. Other players are encouraged to keep going and to respond realistically to the new ideas, actions and comments made by the incoming person. A tagging arrangement has the advantage of spreading the stress and anxiety caused by being "on the firing line" in a role-play. The partner who is sitting out will have a more objective view of what is happening in the role-play, and has the opportunity to devise alternative ways of responding to events. When she is tagged, these ideas can be tried out. Partners can tag each other more than once so that both players get a temporary break. For the other participants, a tagging arrangement enriches the role-play by demonstrating two approaches to the situation. Tagging can also be combined with time-outs.

- **Time-outs**

   A role-play can be "paused" in mid-action to create a time-out. The action stops and a person who is struggling in the role-play has the opportunity, for a few minutes, of getting advice and help about what to do from someone outside the role-play. This might be a tag partner, the trainer, or a support group. This artificial method of freezing time to create a breathing space is possible in role-plays and enables participants to plan what to do next. Time-outs may result in a tag partner swapping places with the person in trouble. You need to make clear who can call for a time-out—usually the person being supported, the support group, or the trainer. While a time-out is in progress, other players are not expected to remain as statues, but it is helpful if the trainer asks them to recall what they were doing, saying or thinking when the time-out was called. This is then used as a prompt when the play resumes. Players should avoid discussing the action during time-outs because it might alter what happens next.

- ## Video Recording

  Using a camcorder to record a role-play on videotape is one of the most effective ways of debriefing the action. "The camera never lies" and it captures gestures and comments that might otherwise go unnoticed. Take precautions in using video cameras because they can inhibit participants. It is good practice to obtain players' consent before filming. Using a video camera with the group before it is used to record a role-play is also helpful in overcoming the natural fears most people have about being exposed on TV. Take care not to show any videotape made of other groups, and to explain that the tape will be erased after use with this group. Asking a volunteer from the group to operate the camera can be another way of reducing the tension surrounding its use. When used in the debriefing session, the video recording should be paused at significant moments when any participant wants to comment on what is happening. Discussion of the videotape easily doubles or triples the time taken to run the role-play itself.

Other Forms of Role-play Techniques

To this point, we have used a common model of role-play to describe the re-creation of a typical situation occurring in real life to which players have to behave or respond. A creative approach to role-play techniques enables them to be used in various other ways; for example, in holding debates or in reaching a decision. Some of these techniques are described in the sections on **Psychodrama** and **Simulation** methods (pages 93 and 131).

Suitability As is evident from the length of this technique's description, role-plays require considerable preparation and forethought. They also require substantial running time and a high degree of trust among group members. For these reasons, role-plays are unsuitable to use with short-life groups or ones with a high turnover. For groups willing to stay together long enough to fully engage in this work and take risks in sharing experiences and skills, role-play can be one of the most powerful learning techniques available.

Rounds

30

Purpose   Rounds offer a quick, simple method of gathering instant reactions and feedback from all participants in a group to a current issue.

Method   When the group leader wishes to hear the views of everyone in the group, she calls for a round. The trainer asks the group a straightforward question, or seeks a reaction to a particular subject. Each person in the group answers in turn, usually in some natural order, such as from left to right or from front to back of the group. Each person speaks without interruption from the others. For rounds to work, explain a few simple rules in advance and enforce them where necessary:

- each person will have an opportunity to respond in turn;
- each person will be listened to respectfully;
- responses should be honest and constructive;
- there will be no discussion about each person's contribution; and
- if discussion is necessary, it will occur at the end of the round after everyone has spoken.

Rounds are often complete in themselves, requiring no further follow-up. However, if participants have asked questions by as part of a round, or if the information derived from a round suggests that more discussion or clarification is required from the group leader, it may be necessary to encourage further open discussion in the whole group.

Rounds are a useful device for opening up a group and encouraging greater participation by more members. They are used by many leaders and trainers as a way of receiving quick feedback from participants. The main benefit of rounds is that they permit each person to make a response. This has two advantages: It creates an opening for the quieter or more withdrawn members to make a contribution, and it forces the louder or more dominant group members to take a back seat for a time.

Examples of the technique   Rounds can be used on many occasions in a group or training event. Here are a few examples:

- to enable each participant to introduce himself by stating his name and reason for attending;
- to allow each person to give his personal response to an awkward situation;
- to seek and receive feedback about the course from each participant; and
- to check how willing participants are to continue with the group or to take a break.

Rounds. . .

Possible variations
A way of making rounds short and quick is to structure the responses being sought. For example, if the trainer wishes to know how much participants are enjoying the group, or have understood the last part of the program, she can call for a round in which "each person responds with a simple score between 1, meaning "not at all", and 5, meaning "a lot". This round is conducted quickly and provides instant information.

Rounds are often used to gather feedback, and further examples are provided in Chapter 4.

Suitability
Rounds are simple, easy to use and to understand, nonthreatening, engage everyone, and can be used with any group.

Sculpting

31

Purpose Most of us are familiar with statue games from childhood. Sculpting exercises use and adapt this technique to provide a nonverbal means of looking at situations. Sculptures are a particularly effective way of examining relationships among people and of building staff teams. The methods described here draw heavily on ideas developed in psychodrama and similar approaches in personal-development work.

Method Sculpting uses different people in a group to represent physically either themselves or other people. The person doing the placing—the "director" of the sculpture—arranges people in the room in relation to one another. The director may also give each person an expression or gesture. Placing several people together in a sculpture gives a dynamic interpretation of the relationships among them, as perceived by the director. The exercise is normally conducted without comment from the participants, except the director, until the sculpting is finished and there is an opportunity to debrief.

A typical sequence in creating a group sculpture is as follows:

- The purpose of the exercise is explained in the context of the group's aims. Because of the potentially threatening nature of many sculptures, it is desirable to give as much information as possible about how it will work and how it will be used. Members of the group should agree to this sort of exercise.

- One person volunteers to direct the sculpture. Depending on the group, this task may be shared by two people. Everyone else sits to one side of the room and a space is cleared in the middle.

- The director takes one participant and places him in the space. The participant may be told to sit or stand, to look in a particular direction, or to appear to be doing something. Simple props may be used if they are at hand. The participant may be given an expression or gesture. Whatever posture is given to any of the participants in the sculpture, the director is responsible for showing how she perceives these individuals in relation to one another (within the context depicted by the group sculpt). Participants are *not* expected to *agree* with this perception or interpretation—that can be discussed later during the debriefing.

- The director takes the second participant and places or arranges the person in some relationship to the first. All sorts of possibilities arise:
  — the physical distance between them may reflect their closeness;
  — the stances towards one another may reflect their perceived relationship;
  — the gestures towards each other may suggest their attitude;
  — the way in which they look at, or avoid, each other, may hint at their feelings;
  — and so on.

  Remember that at this stage the arrangement reflects the director's view only. The participants do not have to agree with it.

- Other participants are added to the group sculpture in the same manner until it is complete.

- If appropriate, the director may place herself in the sculpture as a final component, again without comment.

- When everyone is in place, the whole picture can be captured on video or in a Polaroid® photograph. This may help to show relationships during the subsequent debriefing.

- Each person should have an opportunity to talk about the position they were given. This may result in questions to the director—"Why did you give me this expression?"—or comments—"I felt very awkward when you placed me so close to my manager; this is not how I feel at all."

- The debriefing will normally need to be continued as a group after participants have moved away from their sculpting position. Allow plenty of time for this. As a rule of thumb, the debriefing will take between one and two times the length of time the sculpture took to create. Each person should have the opportunity to talk about how the sculpting felt, and how they feel it compares to their own perception of relations among people.

- Watch out for the expression of strong feelings, and be prepared to deal with them in the group. This is particularly likely if there have been tensions among participants in the "real world" and if these have not been adequately communicated in the past. Rather than attempting to cover up or minimize such emotions and feelings, the value of the exercise lies in giving them scope to be expressed and the underlying issues dealt with properly and fully. In such situations, allow even more time for the debriefing: in groups with a substantial history of miscommunication or pent-up feelings, this may take several hours.

- On some occasions, it is worth repeating the exercise with another volunteer acting as the director. This permits a comparative view of the situation to be shown. Again, a debriefing is required, although this time it may be shorter.

Group sculptures can unlock strong feelings and reactions in a group. One reason for this is that the technique relies upon nonverbal expressions. Without verbal explanations and interpretations, the technique focuses attention on body language and gesture, which tend to be exaggerated to convey the sense of what is happening. Participants are often confronted with a newly discovered awareness of relationships, or they see things in the course of the exercise that they would not normally have time to notice.

To help maintain the focus of the exercise, keep in mind several key points:

- During the sculpting, only the director speaks; other participants refrain from questioning, objecting or clarifying until the debriefing session.

- While the sculpture reflects the director's perception of the situation, he or she cannot be "blamed" for it; if the situation exists (whether people want to recognize it or not), it exists independently of the director depicting it.

- During the debriefing, justifications should be avoided; questions, clarifications and explanations may be necessary, but the point is to help people understand the situation and decide what they want to do about it.

- Watch out for scapegoating, avoidance, and flights into trivia during the debriefing, all of which are ways of denying the validity of the relationships shown by the sculpture.

Examples of the technique

- During a team-building session following a rather uncomfortable period in relations between members of the team, the trainer realized that most people were very good at verbalizing and explaining what had been happening, but that this was not helping everyone come to terms with it. She decided to change the format of the session by using a group sculpture. The trainer asked if the group would agree to participate and invited a volunteer other than the team leader to create the sculpture (the team leader had a particular position of power in the group). One staff member, with some trepidation, arranged his team colleagues in the sculpture. This revealed a strong alliance between two team members who were undermining others, including the team leader. One person in particular was seen to be ostracized by many other team members and had little commitment to working with them. During a lengthy debriefing session, some of the underlying causes of this situation were addressed. Until this had been done, the existing relationship among team members was always going to get in the way of any genuine team building.

Sculpting. . .

- A residents' group had formed a committee. They recognized their relative inexperience at organizing themselves collectively and representing the group's views to outside bodies. They also knew that unless they did organize, they would not be taken seriously. Many group members felt shy about saying what they could do or wanted to do, yet most knew something about the others. With encouragement from a facilitator, the group agreed to create a sculpture with the aim of demonstrating some of their talents. Two members volunteered to work together as directors. They placed participants in different positions and gave them exaggerated characteristics to demonstrate some of their perceived strengths and abilities. During the debriefing, members were willing to be more forthcoming about their interests and competences, having had them recognized by their peers. As a result, the most suitable people were chosen to lead each of the main tasks of the committee.

Possible variations

Group sculpting techniques can be varied to suit different circumstances and needs. Some of these are outlined here, but it is comparatively easy to invent others.

Before-and-after Sculptures

This involves the use of two group sculptures, one showing the relationships among participants now and one as people would like the situation to be in future. The differences between the two can be listed. These differences represent the agenda for change faced by the group. This approach defines "what" needs to be done; only the subsequent discussion will produce ideas for "how" it will be done.

Dynamic Sculptures

Various ways have been developed in which sculptures, rather than depicting a static picture of group relations at one particular moment, can present a more dynamic view of change over time. One such approach involves creating a series of tableau sculptures, each focusing on a critical point in the evolution of the group. A variation of this, requiring substantial direction from the trainer, is as follows.

The trainer acts as the director. He asks the earliest team member to come forward to describe his views of the team on joining and his aspirations for the new work at that time. The events leading up to the arrival of the second person are described. The director then invites this second person to come forward and create a sculpture of the first two people. The second person then describes the situation he found on arrival and his hopes for the work; the first person can respond. Events leading up to the arrival of the third person are described. The director then invites the third person to create a new sculpture. . . and so on up to the present time. Where someone has left, a nonparticipant in the sculpture may stand in for him. Although very time-consuming—such dynamic sculptures can take several hours to complete—they are often very helpful in demonstrating how situations have arisen and in clearing up volumes of miscommunication and myth in a group.

Sculpting and Other Nonverbal Techniques

Sculpting techniques rely on nonverbal communication for their effectiveness. In this respect they are similar to **Drawing** techniques described on page 61. They serve many of the same purposes and can achieve similar outcomes. Drawing techniques are generally perceived as less threatening and easier to explain. Sculpting techniques require more exposure — particularly on the part of the director — and therefore more careful preparation for the group.

Suitability   Before using sculpting methods, trainers and facilitators should think carefully about the degree of risk and exposure involved for participants, and the length of time required to conduct the sculpt and its debriefing, particularly if strong feelings and reactions are revealed. While some would argue that the technique requires a fair degree of perceptual ability and rationalizing skill among group members, others would not agree.

In many respects, young people can engage in the exercise rapidly and effectively for the very reason that they often behave spontaneously. As with role-play methods, these risks should serve as warnings rather than deterrents to using the technique. With many groups it is a most effective device for moving the group beyond an impasse.

Self-assessment Activities

32

Purpose   Self-assessment activities comprise techniques in which group members are invited to reflect on and assess their own level of skill, knowledge or awareness. Self-assessment is often carried out during the introductory part of a session. It is done to focus the group's attention on the topic and to inform the trainer about the existing level of ability. Self-assessments can also be part of a subsequent evaluation of what has been gained from a topic. Self-assessments are rarely objective or comparable in a quantifiable way, because one person's view of his own abilities is based on different criteria and experience than another person's. They are unlikely to share a common baseline.

Method   At their simplest, any small group given the task of sharing and comparing participants' experiences on a specific topic is engaged in a form of self-assessment. More commonly, self-assessment activities involve people working individually. They use a structured exercise to direct their attention toward different aspects of the topic. There are various ways to do this.

Structured Questionnaire

The trainer prepares and copies a list of questions for completion by each participant on the chosen topic. For self-assessment purposes, the questionnaire will probably contain open-ended questions. These invite the respondent to think broadly about the topic and draw on his past experience and knowledge. For some training courses, self-assessments may be distributed to participants in advance as part of course preparation. For more ideas, see the sections on **Questionnaires** and **Homework** (pages 97 and 75).

Rating Scales

Rating scales provide a structured means of assessing existing knowledge, skill or awareness. They use the simple device of a continuum line between two defined and opposite ends. This line forms a scale. The person completing the exercise marks an "X" on the line according to his assessment of that ability. You may prepare several such rating scales on one sheet, each assessing a different aspect of the topic.

Little experience |—+—+—+—+—+—+—| Much experience

A variation is to invite participants to write something about their own rating on each scale on the sheet. A template series of rating scales on the following page can be adapted for your own purposes.

Sentence-completion Exercises

A prepared sheet with sentence "stems" to be completed by each participant can be used as a semistructured assessment technique. Each sentence refers to a different aspect of the topic. For more suggestions about these methods, please turn to the sections on **Sentence-completion Exercises** and **Dialog Books** (pages 127 and 51).

Possible variations

Distribute copies of a rating schedule or questionnaire to members of a group. Ask them to complete the sheet with their assessment of one member of the group. The assessments are then fed back to the member concerned, in a constructive way. This helps people to learn more about how they are perceived. It is a clear example of the feedback mechanism described in the **Johari's Window** model in Chapter 2 (page 13).

Some self-assessment rating scales can be enhanced if the trainer asks each person not only to show their current assessment of themselves on each scale but also to mark some indication of a "desirable" position to be in or to attain. The difference between "actual" and "desirable" points then forms material for discussion and action by the group members.

Suitability

Self-assessment methods are usually easy to prepare and are a useful prompt for introducing a subject and for summarizing what has been gained at the end. They provoke critical thought among participants and a graphic reminder of some of the key points relating to the subject under consideration.

Mark with an "x" on each line how you would assess your own knowledge, skill or awareness with reference to the two extremes given for each scale.

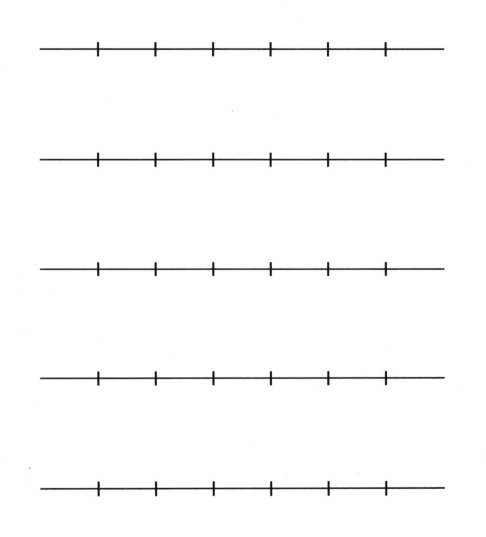

By reflecting on these different scales, how would you summarize your own strengths and weaknesses?

_____

_____

_____

Sentence-completion Exercises

33

Purpose Sentence-completion exercises are structured techniques that can prompt thinking in a group and for assessment purposes. They can be carried out verbally or as pencil-and-paper exercises.

Method The group leader prepares a series of sentence "stems" that participants will complete. A sentence stem comprises the first part of a sentence, with the last part left blank. The sentence stem always indicates the subject or issue that is being looked at, which provides the leader some control over the exercise. The completion of the sentence by each individual participant is less structured, because the stem provides a prompt to which each person will respond differently.

Sentence completion exercises tend to take the form: "A book I have read recently is. . ." or "My preferred career choice is. . . ."

By preparing a worksheet of sentence stems on a related topic, the group leader can focus attention on particular issues. When such worksheets are completed by individuals, they may be used for assessment purposes. As an alternative, the exercise can be completed verbally in small groups. The sentence stem prompts discussion and debate.

Examples of the technique
- In a group designed to build self-esteem and assertiveness skills, the leader wanted to encourage participants to share their experiences with each other. He prepared a series of sentence stems on separate cards that were given to the participants working in small groups. The sentences included:

  The last time I felt inferior was. . .

  I often find myself giving in when. . .

  I find it difficult to complain when. . .

  The person I have most difficulty being assertive with is. . .

  These stems provoked discussion and suggestions from participants that were used later by the group when rehearsing practical skills.

- A teacher working with a group of disinterested students had difficulty encouraging them to articulate their problems because they were not used to reasoning and explaining. He decided to use a sentence-completion exercise as a way of gathering basic information about the experiences of each student. He prepared a worksheet that included the following:

The last time I missed classes was. . .

The reason was. . .

The part of school I like best is. . .

The person I trust most in the school is. . .

The thing I would like to change about my school is. . .

The things I find hard at school include. . .

When each student had completed a worksheet anonymously, they were collected, shuffled and redistributed. Each student held a worksheet completed by another student. The teacher then introduced each question again and invited the students to comment from the worksheets they each held. Inevitably this led into a more-personal discussion, although the hesitant students could protect themselves by referring to the anonymity of each worksheet.

Possible variations

As well as using sentence completions in worksheets and as prompts to verbal discussions, they can be written on separate poster sheets and mounted around the walls of the room for participants to add public comments to with marker pens or sticker memos. The **Talking Wall** (page 177) is an example of this variation.

A similar way of looking at difficulties by referring to particular incidents is provided by **Situation Cards** (page 139).

Use the technique to consider the consequences of particular events or actions in the future. Here, the sentence stem takes the form: "What if. . ." before the event is described. The response indicates how the participant would react. The effect of consequences can be illustrated by linking together a series of "What if. . ." prompts as follows:

What would happen if [*insert event*]?

If that [*add response*] happened, what would that mean for you?

And if that [*insert last response*] happened, what do you think would happen next?

Continue in similar way as far as necessary.

Another version of sentence-completion techniques is to pass messages among members of a group in a more formal way. This is explored more fully as a coworking technique in Chapter 5. Essentially, the message sheet is a memo from one person in the group to another and contains prompt sentences such as:

I would like it if you would start or do more. . .

It would help me if you would do less. . .

Something I would like us both to do is. . .

Suitability   Sentence-completion techniques are particularly useful when working with young people or other groups who may not feel confident about making contributions in a group and for whom a prompt of this nature is a helpful introductory aid. They are quick to prepare and use.

Simulations

34

Purpose

A simulation describes an activity that attempts to replicate or illustrate the main dynamics of a complex situation in which several groups of people or processes interact with each other. Simulations often appear to be large-scale role-plays in which a substantial number of participants take on a range of roles to create a demonstration of what might happen. Some trainers suggest that in role-plays, each person is acting a part, while in a simulation, each person is being himself.

A simulation may be used to examine how people or processes might react given certain events or constraints. The main benefit of the simulation is that it is artificial. Although the processes are designed to be as close as possible to the real thing, they are still controlled within an exercise format. Experimentation is encouraged. The simulation can be stopped at any time, either to prevent unwanted outcomes or to debrief the events and processes that have occurred.

Method

Most simulations require a substantial amount of preparation and direction to be successful. This is the trainer's responsibility. Inadequate preparation often confuses the participants about their roles and makes the exercise itself less productive and relevant than intended.

Many of the methods and considerations that apply to role-plays are equally applicable to simulations, and a careful study of that technique is strongly recommended before a simulation is attempted. One of the major differences between the two is that simulations usually require more participants because the scale of the event being created is larger. This has consequences for the amount of time a simulation requires both to run and to debrief: Many simulations take a minimum of two to three hours to run and up to a full day to complete with an adequate debriefing of all participants. The main steps for the trainer to organize are described below.

- The simulation requires a clear focus. What is the situation the simulation will recreate? What processes involved in this situation is the simulation designed to illustrate?

Examples of typical simulations include:

— studying how different parts of a production system within an organization relate to one another;

— examining how communications do or do not work among different teams or staff groups;

— modeling how decisions are made across different levels of a management structure;

— testing the likely chain of events resulting from a particular event (such as an accident or new initiative);

— posing "what-if" questions to examine the possible consequences of different future events.

• Be sure to identify each of the groups or individuals within the simulation. They form the characters for participants taking part. The extent to which each must be described depends on the knowledge participants already have of each of these characters. The greater the degree of description attached to each role, the closer the simulation may come to represent reality. By the same token, the greater the description of the role, the lower the scope for creativity and inventiveness by participants in developing the role.

• Prepare a full set of written descriptions, or *briefs*. Depending on the nature of the simulation, different sorts of briefs will be required:

Overall Brief

This is a short description of the overall simulation, which is issued to each participant. It sets out the purpose of the exercise and establishes the general scene. The overall brief may list each of the group and individual roles within the simulation. It should set out the rules for conducting the activity, including the role of the director, how to ask questions in mid-event, and how the simulation is to end.

Role Briefs

These describe the main characteristics and behaviors of each of the individuals and groups within the simulation. Usually, participants may only see their own role briefs before the simulation begins. The role brief may describe the position and authority of the group, how it relates to others and the things it considers important.

Action Briefs

These notes inform each role group of what they should attempt to achieve through the simulation. Often the action brief forms part of the role brief but, in complex simulations, the two need to be issued separately. Groups and individuals receive their role brief and are given time to think themselves into the role. Later, they are given an action brief informing them of what they are to do within the simulation. The action briefs set the simulation in motion.

- Check the practical requirements for the simulation. Different groups may need to operate from different rooms. Each will need a table and chairs. Ways of communicating among groups must be established and checked: written notes, internal telephones, people moving between rooms, and so on. In simulations with six or more groups in different places, a layout map with labels attached to the rooms or spaces occupied by different groups may be helpful.

- Having completed the preparation work, introduce the simulation to the training group, carefully explaining its purpose, structure and method. Invariably there will be questions that need to be answered fully.

- The ground rules for the simulation should be set out for everyone to understand. There are no standard ground rules, but points to consider and cover in the ground rules may include:

  — whether participation is compulsory or voluntary;

  — whether people can choose their roles or will have them assigned;

  — the confidentiality of the exercise;

  — the limits to what people can say and do to each other within the simulation itself;

  — how participants can express their disapproval or dissent at what is happening within the simulation;

  — how the simulation can be stopped, and who is responsible for this; and

  — what will happen when the simulation ends.

- Allocate or select individual and group roles. The choice depends on the purpose of the simulation. If it is designed to illustrate a potential future event (as, for example, a major accident) participants should normally be allocated their real-life role. In a simulation examining present-day communication issues within an established organization, it may be more productive for participants to be allocated roles randomly so that few people end up with their own real-life role: In this way, the simulation will illustrate participants' perceptions of each other's communication.

- Having distributed the overall, role and action briefs, give each group time to read the material and prepare the role.

- The trainer, now working as the "director" of the simulation, announces the start. Each group and individual should now attempt to put their action brief into effect.

- The trainer/director must have no direct part to play in the simulation. He will be monitoring what is going on, moving among the different groups to gain an overall impression of the action and remaining alert to any incidents of ground rules being broken. While the trainer remains outside the action, he will have to use his own judgment to enforce ground rules, provide answers to questions about the process itself, and respond constructively to unexpected events. In simulations that engage participants on an emotional level, the trainer should expect strong reactions from players. It is not the trainer's role to prevent these or diffuse them while the simulation is running, but the trainer is responsible for protecting the physical safety of all participants and for ensuring that all such incidents are fully and adequately discussed during the post-simulation debriefing.

- The trainer must announce a formal ending to the simulation to everyone involved. This may occur when the action brief has been fulfilled or at the end of a preset time period. Occasionally the trainer will stop the simulation before its natural end because participants are in danger of becoming hurt or over-involved in the process, and the possibility needs to be avoided by ending it immediately.

- As with any role-play, all participants need time and assistance to "come out of role" before moving on to the next stage. Several methods for doing this are described in the **Role-play** section, which begins on page 103. Most involve participants talking with others about topics other than the simulation: reaffirming who they really are, describing matters of personal importance, removing physical labels and name-tags describing their assumed role. In most cases, it helps to physically move participants away from the rooms in which the simulation occurred to a "neutral" space for the debriefing.

- The debriefing will take at least as much time as the simulation took to run. In most instances, the debriefing should be given twice as much time. The debriefing requires a carefully planned structure controlled by the trainer. Depending on the nature of the simulation and the actual events that occurred, the debriefing will need to cover:

— whether the action briefs were achieved;

— the factors that helped or hindered their achievement;

— what each individual or group experienced or felt during the simulation about their own role (this takes considerable time to do properly, as each individual or group needs sufficient time to explain their respective point of view while the others listen);

— what each individual or group experienced or said regarding other's roles (again, needing considerable time and sensitivity to explore fully);

— the implications of these insights — what people have learned, what they need to do or change in their work as a result of the simulation, how they might react or behave differently in future;

— the conclusions and action points from the simulation which may need to be formally recorded; and

— a final opportunity for each participant to express any remaining feelings, anxieties, frustrations or comments arising from the simulation that have not been adequately dealt with up to now.

Examples of the technique

As suggested above, simulations can be devised to suit many applications. Here are a number of illustrations.

- Where several different organizations or agencies, each with their own priorities and policies, are expected to collaborate and work together, perhaps on a joint project, a simulation can be used to model how key players from each agency might function in relation to each other. The overall brief identifies one manageable aspect of the project as the focus for the exercise. Each participant plays him- or herself. The action briefings set out particular goals to be achieved by each of the player groups or individuals. During the debriefing, the extent to which cooperation occurred during the simulation can be examined and lessons drawn about how real collaboration can be achieved in the actual project.

- Disaster simulations form a specific type of interagency or collaborative exercise. Here, different players represent their own organizations. The overall briefing sets out details of a particular disaster that has just occurred. Each of the agencies must now respond, preferably in cooperation with each other, towards the common goal of responding to the disaster. How they work together, what inhibits the process, how communication develops, will all evolve during the simulation and need to be discussed in the extensive debriefing.

- Personal styles of authority and communication can be illustrated by an artificial simulation. In this case, the overall briefing is invented purely for the exercise but requires all the players to relate to one another. Each participant is given a role relevant to the situation but outside his normal experience. A common example is a simulation involving the production of a newspaper or a TV news program. Each person is allocated a role (editor, reporter, member of public, artist, cameraman, and so on). A series of news stories is given to the group by the trainer in the form of past newspaper cuttings. The group, in role, must prepare a news broadcast or pasted-up copy of a newspaper within a set time—perhaps 75 minutes—when the simulation ends. The result is usually frantic activity as people come to grips with unfamiliar roles and cope with the task and its deadline. Whether the task is achieved is almost immaterial. The ensuing debriefing will reveal a great deal about how individual participants exercise their authority and style of communication during the exercise and, by extension, in their real-life work.

Possible variations

Simulations can be used creatively in many learning situations either to model what already happens between people, or what might happen in some hypothetical situation. The crux of the simulation is the dynamic process it generates and how this is understood by participants and used to influence their future behavior and actions. The trainer can introduce a number of additional features, which may enhance the event.

One or more video cameras can be used to record either the working of key groups within the simulation or to prepare a collage of small episodes taken from each of the different groups at various times. Although this will add to the debriefing time, the video illustrates clearly what went on in each group. Remember that participants are likely to only see the working of their own role group and that they have no opportunity to experience the processes within other role groups at first hand.

To make the simulation more unpredictable—as would tend to occur in real life—the trainer can introduce "random events" as the event proceeds. Random factors consist of specific events that take place suddenly and may influence how the role groups respond. Random factors need to be tailored to the context of the situation. They may be serious or humorous. Examples include the arrival of an important company executive, a change in political power, a sudden change in the weather, a new policy directive. These events may be announced verbally by the trainer, or introduced through a "newspaper" quickly prepared and copied by the trainer on site. While random factors can add realism to the simulation and often provide a measure of relief, they can also irritate participants and may be counter-productive. Limit their use.

Some simulations may involve 40 or more players. They are extensive logistical exercises to run, control and debrief. This is a daunting task for any trainer. Depending on the size and complexity of the group, most simulations are best run by two or three trainers working together and coordinating the process. While one person may be the overall designer of the exercise, the others need to be properly briefed about its aims and structure so all trainers are working to the same end.

Suitability   Simulations have great potential in training and learning events where participants work together long enough to develop confidence in each other. They are often underused because of the amount of preparation required, the scale of the exercise and its unpredictability. Don't underestimate these factors! Trainers need time, energy and confidence to put on a successful simulation. However, neither should these factors deter experimentation with a technique that often has a large and powerful influence over the learning of group members. As with role-play, a simulation offers an opportunity to re-create, experiment with and analyze processes and events that are happening anyway. The creation by the trainer of a safe and protected environment in which such learning can take place offers people a medium in which to try different approaches and new responses. This can make a dramatic difference in the way they behave and react back in the real world.

Situation Cards

35

Purpose   This technique uses index cards or Post-Its® to present participants with specific examples of real-life situations they may encounter. It encourages participants to react to each example by expressing their feelings or discussing what they would do next in that event.

Method   A series of specific examples or situations is prepared by the trainer in advance relevant to the topic under discussion by the group. Each situation is written on a separate index card. Cards often take the form of:

"What would you do if. . . ?"

"How would you feel if. . . ?"

"What would your response be if. . . ?"

Participants work together in groups of five or six. Each group has a set of cards, which can be distributed to the participants or left face-down in a central pile. The first card is read aloud by one member, who responds by saying how he or she would respond to that situation. Other members of the group are encouraged to add their reactions or responses and to suggest further alternatives. Depending on the nature of the issue, the group may want to debate alternative strategies for handling the situation until a preferred response is reached or greater confidence is generated. The next card is then read aloud and the process repeated.

Examples of the technique

- In a course designed to increase participants' confidence in handling awkward situations, the trainer distributed a series of situation cards describing different incidents to small groups. The trainer asked each group to discuss the best way of responding to the incidents.

- A group was discussing different options for the future development of a project. To clarify the implications of each option, the leader prepared a series of situation cards. Each card depicted a possible future event arising from one of the options. In discussing their reactions to these potential situations, the group developed insights into the implications of the options they currently faced.

Situation cards. . .

Possible variations

There is an alternative to presenting participants with a prepared set of situation cards. When a group is working well together, they can be invited to write out their own situation cards based upon real events they have encountered or situations they fear they might meet. These can be prepared anonymously if participants so wish. They can be written in block letters, with names and other distinguishing information removed or disguised. The cards prepared by the group are collected, shuffled and distributed for discussion.

This variation works particularly well with subject matter that is sensitive and personal. The cards enable participants to reveal anxieties or personal difficulties without having to identify themselves directly. In this way, they can "test" the reaction of other group members and, it is hoped, gain group support for the predicament.

Suitability

Situation cards are suitable for a wide range of groups and almost all ages. They work well when participants can get together in subgroups to share ideas and reactions. This requires a level of trust and confidence among participants that may not be present until the group is established. Confidential issues can be tackled through situation cards if the cards are presented without information identifying the original author or subject.

Small Groups

36

Purpose

Many users of this *Tool Kit* will already be working with small groups as the context for applying these techniques. But remember that the deliberate use of smaller groups when working with larger groups is also an option. Small-group work permits participants to engage more fully in the learning process. It may encourage those who are more reticent to contribute as a consequence of the perceived safety and confidentiality of the smaller group.

Method

There is no established size for a *small* group. Whatever size group you are working with, you may always request the whole group to break up into smaller units for specific tasks. In general, this is referred to as "splitting into smaller groups." Pairs or triads are specific forms of small groups. Techniques for those are discussed elsewhere in this chapter. In this section, small groups are assumed to include four to eight participants.

Inviting participants at an event to break into smaller groups serves two main purposes. It allows a greater range of tasks to be accomplished if each small group is given a different task. Or it enables more participants to contribute to the discussion if each group is engaged in the same task. Thus, small-group work is a method of encouraging participation and for achieving a higher output.

This is achieved at the expense of some of the trainer's control over the whole group. When everyone is working together, the trainer is capable of exercising the maximum control over the group by directing the discussion or task and moderating the process. The more that people work separately or in smaller groups, the harder it is for the trainer to maintain control over the process. The trainer can set the initial task and bring it to an end, but he or she is physically unable to take part in all the simultaneous small groups. Often, this is the point of using the technique: It permits participants to explore issues without the presence of the trainer. Such situations are desirable if the subject matter requires a high degree of confidentiality or if participants are encouraged to discuss their own personal and varied responses to a topic without any one view prevailing.

Groups can be divided into smaller groups on a self-selecting basis or more deliberately by the trainer. Trainer selection may be preferred if you wish to ensure a particular mix of participants (or to engineer group membership in some way). Self-selection by participants may feel more comfortable for them, because they will tend to gravitate towards people they know or have some affinity towards. Simple methods for creating arbitrary mixes in small groups include numbering participants. For example, people are numbered 1–2–3–4–1–2–3–4–1 and so on, around the large group. All the "ones" get together, all the "twos" form a small group, and so on. Or you can impose a condition on small-group membership—such as no two people from the same work setting in any group.

A problem for the trainer is what to do when everyone else is working in small groups. There is often a strong desire to check up on each small group to "make sure they are doing it properly." Try to avoid this. The purpose of small groups is to let them do the task on their own. This does not mean refusing to help. When small groups begin their task, the trainer should be available to clarify the instructions and to offer assistance to any group requesting it. When small groups are up and running (detectable by the level of conversation and the visible signs of activity), the trainer should remain in the background and tune in discreetly to different small-group discussions from a distance. Unless it is unavoidable, the trainer should not participate directly in any small group discussion or task. Trainer participation inhibits the group members, who inevitably tend to take their lead from the trainer's comments in such situations.

Watch for the possibility that one or more ineffective small groups will form. This may happen if one participant in the small group is dominant, scapegoated, avoided, or made to appear different. Other participants may avoid joining a small group involving such a person, or resent being part of such a group. To forestall this situation, either work separately with the individual to help him participate effectively, or regularly change the composition of the small groups so everyone is part of an effective group for most of the time.

Avoid situations in which lots of small groups are formed, each doing the same task. This can be boring and repetitive, particularly if each group is expected to offer feedback in a subsequent plenary session. Instead, give small groups different topics and tasks to work on that represent all aspects of the main issue.

When several small groups are engaged in giving feedback to a larger group, it can be interesting and stimulating to invite them to use more creative forms of feedback than just a verbal report.

Creative feedback techniques for small groups include:

- using mime rather than words;

- making a dramatic presentation of the conclusions;

- reporting the key points in the form of a debate between two or more members of the small group; and

- writing key points on large poster sheets attached to the wall and inviting people to walk around and read the ideas before asking questions.

Examples of the technique

- During a training event on management skills, the trainer gave a short presentation outlining several management theories. The group then divided into smaller groups, each composed of participants from different work settings, who were asked to consider the applicability of the different theories by drawing on their own experiences with management at work.

- A staff group was planning to introduce a major new project into their workplace. Working together, the staff drew up a large list of topics that needed to be discussed before the project could be implemented. The group decided to break up into smaller groups, each focusing on a different topic. The small groups were self-selecting in membership, with staff members joining the group that would best use their expertise. Each small group focused on one topic, decided on recommendations for proceeding and reported its findings to the whole group.

- A group of people meeting regularly over a long period of time to support each other in coping with a difficult medical condition suddenly lost one of their members after a short illness. To explore how each person felt about this bereavement, the group spent some time in smaller groups in which everyone was able to talk about what the loss meant to them. The intimate nature of the smaller groups encouraged people to reveal more of their true feelings — and gave each person more time to talk. The process of grieving was helped as a result.

Possible variations

Small groups are often a starting point for moving into more participative or experiential work with a group. The format is often combined with other techniques described in this *Tool Kit* to achieve particular tasks.

Suitability   Small-group work is a common technique in many training events, self-help groups and action groups. In many ways it is similar to a committee that sets up subcommittees to undertake specific responsibilities. Provided the group is sufficiently well established to share a common purpose and commitment (so that the trainer has fewer concerns about losing control of the process), small groups can be used safely and profitably in many situations.

Television and Video

37

Purpose
The use of video filming and recording by a group is described further in the section on **Audio/visual Equipment** on page 28. However, given the huge output of ready-made materials on television, radio and satellite broadcasting, and the easy availability of prerecorded video cassettes, these media should also be considered as a source of interesting and stimulating material for any group.

Participant risk factor **1**

Method
The most obvious use of television and film materials is to locate a program directly related to the topic you wish to consider. Record the program on a personal video recorder for later use, or rent it from a commercial outlet. This can be a hit-or-miss affair. The difficulty of using homemade recordings is that the relevance of a program is often not apparent until part way through—by which time it is too late to record the whole program (unless you know it will be repeated later). Renting prerecorded cassettes, either from a video store or from a company offering training and special-interest films, is risky unless they have a very good catalog describing the suitability of each particular film, or better you have the chance to preview the film.

An alternative is to make your own video using clips from broadcast programs. This overcomes one of the common difficulties in using prerecorded programs—that only a small proportion of the content is relevant to your purposes. The benefit of a video to any group often comes from just a short clip, which can be used as a focus or prompt to wider discussion.

Many TV programs contain material that helps illustrate points you wish to make with a group. By gathering several relevant short clips together on one videotape, you will have a library of examples and prompts to use during a group event. Because each of these is likely to be very short, they will act as triggers and prompts for a longer discussions among group members.

Collating suitable clips on any subject from broadcast TV need not be time-consuming. You will need a copy of the program schedules to identify suitable programs. Rather than recording whole programs, record short illustrative excerpts. When you are not sure which parts to record, you can either check to see if the program is repeated (and then record parts of the repeat) or use two video recorders linked together for simple editing.

Provided the recorded materials are used by you directly and are not rebroadcast or distributed commercially, you are unlikely to infringe the copyright. Do not give copies to participants, as this could lead to copyright problems.

Examples of the technique

- During a training course about health and safety at work, a 30-minute video produced by a safety organization was shown to participants, highlighting key factors.

- As part of a training event about public speaking, the trainer assembled several one- or two-minute clips of TV programs on a videotape to illustrate different presentational styles. These included: a weather forecast, an editorial, a monolog from a play and a news broadcast. Participants were invited to consider the pros and cons of each style.

- In a group discussing personal relationships, the facilitator showed a video recording of a TV program with a panel discussion on the topic. After each panelist had spoken, the trainer stopped the tape and invited group members to react. The videotape was restarted for the next panelist's contribution and again stopped for the group's reaction. In this way, the group could "interact" with the TV panelists and eventually establish their own views.

- During a later session with the same group examining family relationships, the facilitator recorded several short excerpts from a popular TV soap opera. These clips were shown one at a time to prompt discussion about family dynamics and the difficulties of communications within families.

Suitability

TV, film and video recordings can be used with any group, provided that the subject matter and comprehension age is suitable for the intended audience. Shorter clips and programs are better than longer ones. There is a danger of the medium becoming more dominant than the message. Our familiarity with television today is such that many people almost expect to be "spoon-fed" and not to have to do much work themselves. In a training and learning context, television and video material may be a useful aid, but it should not replace the work participants do in thinking about issues and applying to their own situation the knowledge and skills gained.

Triads

38

Purpose
Triads are a particularly effective and supportive form of work with small groups. Developed from a technique first used to practice counseling skills, triads enable group members to explore personal issues, examples or problems in a supportive way, develop or affirm their own action plan, or receive direct feedback on their performance.

Method
Participants are divided into groups of three. If numbers do not work out exactly, it is possible to have some groups of four, but try to avoid pairs. The trainer should not be a member of any triad, because his attention is required to manage the process and the time.

Triad exercises can be used to enable participants to share and discuss specific examples or incidents related to a topic under discussion in the group. Each example is drawn from the personal experience of the person contributing it. In these cases, triads are used to provide support and to help in problem solving if appropriate. Triads help two people rehearse communication skills; the exercise offers direct feedback about the effectiveness of the skills being rehearsed. The beauty of the triads exercise is that each person becomes the focus of the activity in turn, so that everyone is included and has a chance to receive direct support or feedback.

Each member of each triad takes on one of the following roles:

- **Speaker.** This person will provide the issue or example that she wishes to focus on in the exercise.

- **Listener.** This is the person with whom the speaker communicates during the exercise and who responds with support, counsel or advice.

- **Observer.** This person takes no part in the exchange between the speaker and listener but records what occurs and provides either a summary or direct feedback to either party at the end.

These relationships are depicted in the diagram below.

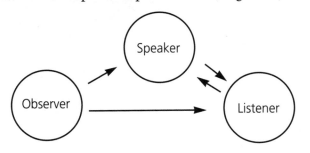

Triad relationships

Each triad works independently in a quiet part of the room. The speaker selects a topic or incident to discuss with the listener. The listener helps the speaker explain and explore the example and derive learning or action points from it. The conversation lasts for a preestablished period of time, perhaps 15 minutes.

At the end of this time, there is a debriefing period of 5 minutes, using the comments from the observer. The comments from the observer will vary depending on the nature of the issue being discussed. The observer may summarize some of the insights gained by the speaker; he may comment on the ability of the listener to offer support; or he may contribute his own comments from an independent viewpoint. During the debriefing period, the speaker and listener may also wish to comment on their experience of the process.

After a short debriefing period, members of the triad change roles. A second person becomes the speaker and repeats the same process with the same time limits. After a further debriefing, the roles change again and the process is repeated for a third time, giving each person the opportunity to experience all three roles.

When all triads have completed their work, the trainer may wish to bring the whole group back together to enable members to comment on insights gained from the exercise or the value of the exercise itself.

Examples of the technique

Triad exercises have been given many uses because of their effectiveness as a learning-and-support technique. Here are a few examples:

- During a counseling-skills course, triads were used to demonstrate and rehearse active-listening communication techniques. The speaker acted as a client seeking counseling help from the listener. The listener practiced the skills of active listening on the speaker. The observer and the speaker provided the listener with feedback about the effectiveness of these skills during the debriefing.

- A group of people developing their training skills were looking at their fears and inhibitions as trainers. They used a triad exercise to give each participant the opportunity to talk about his or her personal fears when training. Each speaker had 15 minutes to talk about his fears, with support and encouragement from a colleague acting as the listener. During the debriefing, the observer was invited to place the speaker's fears in some sort of perspective.

- During a large conference, numerous issues were raised but there had been insufficient time to look at more than a few of them during the workshop sessions. During the final session, the conference organizers decided to use a triad technique. Conference delegates were invited to form triads. Within each triad, each delegate had the opportunity to spend 20 minutes as the speaker, talking about the issue of most concern to him during the conference and what should be done about it. The listener offered help and encouragement. During the debrief, the observer worked with the speaker to define what action the speaker now wanted to take on that issue. In the space of 90 minutes, the conference delegates were able to address a very large number of different issues which the program otherwise did not provide time for.

Possible variations

Triad exercises can be used in a great many situations with almost all groups. Given the positive feedback this exercise usually receives, take opportunities to extend, vary or adapt the basic technique to suit different circumstances.

Suitability

Triads are a powerful and highly supportive technique for encouraging people to explore issues of particular importance to them. Participants are able to control the exercise and use it for their own support and development. It takes considerable time to carry out properly, and triads should not be used unless there is at least 90 minutes of uninterrupted time for completion. It can be a difficult exercise to explain. The three roles need careful elaboration to ensure that each works well. Good timekeeping is essential. There is a tendency for the first round to run long and for the last round to be cut short by a deadline for the whole exercise. To avoid this, the trainer should monitor the time and announce clearly to all triads the point at which they should move on to the debriefing or next round.

Trust Games

39

Purpose   Trust-building exercises have gotten a bad name in many groups—mainly because they have been used inappropriately or conducted improperly. As the name suggests, their function is to build trust and openness among members of a group so the group coheres and develops an improved sense of mutual support and collaborative work.

Method   Before reading about different types of trust activities, consider when they should (and should not) be used. Many trust games rely upon physical activity and contact among members of the group. By nature, they also require one participant to give some control over his or her safety to another. It should be apparent that group members must have some degree of trust one with another and a desire to build more before they attempt further trust-building exercises. Thus trust games can rarely be used at the start of any group session because members have neither the knowledge nor the willingness to engage in such activities with strangers. Trust games should only be considered if they are appropriate to the purpose of the group. The trainer will need to ask: Why is it important for enhanced trust to be established among members? In what way will greater trust help fulfill the group's objectives? How will participants react to the introduction of any such exercise? Some appropriate uses of trust games are suggested in the next section.

A range of trust activities has been devised and the list that follows is only a summary of some of the more common methods. Feel free to devise or substitute others that appear relevant to the purpose and to amend these to suit particular circumstances.

Blindfold Walk

Participants work in pairs. One person in each pair is given a blindfold. The sighted person then leads the blindfolded person around an obstacle course, taking care to ensure she is not hurt. The obstacle course may be outdoors using trees, benches, walls and other features. An indoor obstacle course may use furniture, curtains and doors to create artificial hazards through which the blindfolded person must be maneuvered.

Horizontal Lift

One person agrees to lie supine on the floor (face up), preferably with her eyes closed. Other members of the group numbering not fewer than five or six arrange themselves around the supine member and lift the person into the air by placing their hands underneath the head, shoulders, hips, thighs and knees. The supine person should be encouraged to relax and to let all the weight be carried by the lifters rather than attempt to maintain control by tightening muscles. Depending on the strength and confidence of the lifters, the supine person may be lifted to waist, chest or shoulder height.

Falling Statue

A volunteer agrees to stand upright with eyes closed in the middle of a tightly packed circle comprising eight or so other participants. The volunteer then falls backwards until caught by the person behind. The volunteer should be encouraged to fall naturally and not to control the fall by bending knees or remaining taut. The catcher pushes the volunteer upright again so he then falls in another direction to be caught by someone else. And so on. Initially, the circle will need to be tightly packed so the falling distance is short; as confidence grows, the catchers may be able to enlarge the size of the circle slightly to permit a longer fall.

Blind Run

Furniture is cleared from the room and everyone lines up at one end. Two people move to the other end and stand at some distance in front of the end wall; they hold each other's arms to form a strong human barrier. The first volunteer then starts to run with his eyes closed from one end of the room towards the human wall. The job of the human-wall pair is to stop the runner before he reaches the end of the room— gently. This is a difficult trust activity: Many people will only walk, or slow up dramatically when halfway down the room.

Running Jump

Six people stand together and face opposite each other in three pairs; they hold the arms of their pair partner to create a "bed". A volunteer starts from some distance away, runs towards the end of the "bed" and then dives onto it, to be supported by the six people holding arms. It can be helpful to have a seventh person at the end to catch the head in case the jumper overshoots.

Care is required in introducing any trust game. Among the points to observe are:

- a clear explanation of why enhanced trust among participants is desirable at this point;
- voluntary rather than compulsory participation in any activity;
- attention to special needs or conditions required in order for each individual to take part;
- adequate safeguards to ensure there is no physical risk; and
- adequate controls by the trainer to respond to other participants who may not react in a "trusting" way during an activity.

Examples of the technique

- A group of young people planning an trip together decided to use a series of trust activities at each planning session as a way of learning to rely on one another.

- A mutual-support group for women that had been meeting for some time decided to include trust-building exercises when they realized that some women were withholding information and experiences from the group. They used trust exercises to explore where the problems in confidence and relationships among members lay.

- A group of senior managers had spent two days working out new policies together. Before starting the next session, they agreed to undertake a trust game, partly to change the tempo by introducing a physical activity and partly to build confidence in each other. They realized that, without mutual trust, their ability to implement new policies would be limited.

- A new community-action group comprised representatives of many different organizations with a history of fighting each other. During a retreat weekend together designed to create a united team, the trainer used a series of trust activities to engender a sense of mutual support rather than antagonism.

Possible variations

As already suggested, trust games are rarely suitable at the start of any group session. Instead, a choice of **Icebreaker** or getting-to-know-you techniques may be more appropriate (page 77).

Suitability

Many groups are wary of trust games either because they do not see their relevance or because they are reluctant to expose themselves to apparently foolish behavior in front of others. Trust games are relevant to situations in which participants choose to work more closely together and are willing to do something physical as a way of achieving this. In many groups, developing enhanced trust through such techniques is not appropriate. Only the trainer can assess this, and the group itself needs to be involved in the decision. Trust activities tend to be better received if group members already have some familiarity with each other and have sufficient time together to make closer working relationships beneficial.

Chapter 4
Tools for Evaluation

Evaluation is an important aspect of any work carried out with groups. It provides the trainer or leader with reactions and responses to the event or session that should enable him to learn something and improve his own skills. This is particularly relevant if the program will be repeated in the future. Feedback and evaluation also give participants opportunities to say what has been happening for them: Such comments may be positive or negative. Pleasant and rewarding as it is to receive positive comments, it is often more beneficial to a trainer's professional development to listen to criticism about an event. That way the source of the difficulties can be understood and learning derived from the experience. Because the groups are frequently about learning and development for *participants,* evaluation provides the trainer with a parallel opportunity to learn from the event.

In this chapter we consider various feedback and evaluation techniques. Feedback is an opportunity during the course of an event to take stock of how participants are reacting to it. Many exercises contain a feedback element when, say, small groups report back on their work in a plenary session. In this chapter we will look at techniques that provide feedback about the *whole* event, rather than a specific activity. Many of these methods may be adapted for use at both levels. Any feedback technique stops the group process for a time as participants are invited to comment on what is happening to them, what they have learned, or how they are feeling. Because of this interruption, choose with some care when to ask for feedback. Normally, it would be appropriate to ask at natural breaks in the group program or when the process is flagging. In the latter instance, seeking feedback may provide a way for participants to reenergize the group by expressing any obstacles or problems. It is often good practice to seek feedback halfway through any event. This gives the leader an opportunity to introduce change in the time that remains. Feedback at the end is interesting, but of no use in improving the event for those participants. The primary benefits of any feedback exercise are therefore to:

- encourage participants to evaluate their learning and involvement so far,

- assist the group leader in assessing progress so far and planning the next stage,

- create an opportunity for change to be introduced in the event or program, and

- create an opportunity to reaffirm the event or program.

If feedback provides some form of interim assessment during the life of a group, evaluation techniques should provide a more substantive judgment of the learning and development that has taken place over the life of the group. This may take the form of a "before-and-after" comparison, which assesses the "value added" by the group or course experience. Or, it may focus more subjectively on attitudes, feelings and reactions to the event. One choice that faces the evaluator is whether to carry out the evaluation at the end of the event (when the experience is still fresh without necessarily being consolidated), or whether to wait a while (when recall of the event may have dimmed, but more mature reflection may have taken place). Methods for measuring change in a group in a quantitative manner are often difficult to define. However, it is common to find evaluations of training courses and group exercises that focus on the more qualitative aspects of participants' experience. Whatever form of evaluation is conducted, the main aims should be:

- determining whether the course or group has achieved its purpose;

- identifying what worked, or failed, during the course or event (in both the content and the process), so lessons can be drawn;

- identifying what needs remain to be addressed (or have now arisen) for participants; and

- identifying any further action that is now required.

The sections that comprise this chapter each describe a different group of feedback or evaluation techniques. They are presented in a standard format for easy comprehension. Feel free to adapt techniques to suit your particular circumstances.

Action-plan Reviews

40

Purpose   The review process is a structured way of reexamining plans that were made earlier and assessing the progress made towards implementing them; difficulties can be discussed and the plans amended if necessary.

Method   The review technique is based upon the **Action Plans** generated during the main course or event (see Chapter 3). Participants are invited to a follow-up day and asked to bring their action plans with them. The day is spent on two tasks:

- Participants report back on progress made towards implementation of their action plans, identifying successes and problems along the way.

- At least half the available time is devoted to work on solving problems that have arisen so that participants can leave with renewed commitment or fresh ideas for carrying out their action plans.

The role of the trainer or leader during the review day is to facilitate the event, help participants make sense of their experience, and contribute to the problem-solving sessions. This may involve restating some of the lessons from the original course, but the review day is not designed to introduce new material not previously covered at the event itself.

A part of the review day can be used to evaluate the original event. The trainer can initiate a discussion (or use any of the other methods in this chapter) to gather the views of participants with the benefit of the reflection that has occurred since the original event.

Examples of the technique
- A management group had spent three days working together on a new policy and plans for its implementation. Six months later, they met again for a day to discuss how it was proceeding. Several problems were identified which, by working together, the managers were able to overcome. As a result, the new policy was put back on track.

- A five-day counseling-skills course was followed by a follow-up day two months later, at which participants reported on the use they had been able to make of the skills learned on the course. Several participants reported difficulties and the trainer was able to remind them of key points from the course and to run some short role-plays examining those situations that remained problematic. At the end of the day, the trainer asked for suggestions for improving the whole course.

Suitability   The option of running a review day depends on the opportunity for bringing people together again. Inevitably, some people will drop out, for whatever reason. Attrition can be minimized if the intention of holding a review day is announced at the outset (before the original event takes place) and if the value of action plans is stressed throughout the event.

Assessing Outcomes and Changes

41

Purpose
To produce a more objective evaluation of the work of any group, you must assess and measure outcome. The key to this lies in when and how the outcomes are specified. Any legitimate and objective use of outcomes as an evaluation tool requires the intended outcome to have been established *before* the group meets and then reviewed after the group has completed its work.

Method
Assessing outcomes and changes involves three clear stages: specifying the objectives at the outset; determining how each objective will be measured; and reporting on the final outcome compared to each original objective.

Specifying the Objectives

All assessments of change depend on the specification of objectives at the outset. Objectives spell out what the group, course or event is intended to achieve. The objectives should be as clear and measurable as possible. Examples of specific objectives include:

- all participants achieving a qualified status in the course (where the qualification is awarded by an external body);
- establishing, funding and setting up a particular project;
- solving a specified problem;
- starting and completing a $3,000 fund-raising campaign;
- preventing the building of a new supermarket;
- preparing a report within one month that will be accepted by the board.

Each of these objectives identifies a clear task or intended outcome, which others are able to recognize and assess.

Measuring Each Objective

The initial objectives must be measurable either in a pass/fail sense or according to some assessable numeric scale. In some cases, conditions are attached to the objective, such as time. If the outcome can only be measured in a subjective way (such as, "enabling participants to feel more confident" or "creating an improvement in the environment") it suggests a need to return to the objectives and specify them differently. This is often achieved by breaking down the objective into its component parts or providing examples of what an apparently subjective outcome would mean in practical terms.

Comparing the Final Outcome to Each Original Objective

This is the critical part of the evaluation. Using the measuring instruments defined in the previous stage, the final outcomes are tested against the original objectives. The results establish the success of the session, and measure the degree of change that has taken place. Measurement may be carried out by members of the group, by the leader, or by an external party.

Examples of the technique

- A small service company decided to run a course in "customer relations". Its objective was to cut customer complaints by half. Before running the course, the number and nature of complaints was logged over a two-month period. After running the five-day course, the number and nature of complaints in the following two-month period was logged and compared with the earlier situation.

- Members of a management team had been experiencing problems with their computer system. It was decided to form a small task force to investigate. The group's objective was to look at the problems, consider how they could be solved, and take action within a month to rectify the problems. The outcome was assessed by whether members of the team could get their computers to work properly within the month.

- A quality-circle group met regularly to consider ways of improving the firm's products and production process. The outcome of the group was assessed each year in terms of whether it generated improvements that led to the production of better products (assessed by a consumer panel) at a lower unit cost to the company.

Possible variations

Where the outcomes of a training course are being evaluated, it may be possible to involve the participants' supervisor or manager in the process. The manager may wish to specify the learning outcomes for staff attending the course. Where these involve the acquisition of knowledge or skills, the manager can observe how these are used after the course, and can discuss the outcomes with the participant through ongoing supervision or appraisal meetings.

Suitability

Outcomes and changes can be specified in a wide variety of ways to suit different situations. The knack is in setting down clear and explicit objectives beforehand so they are clear to all concerned and capable of some form of quantitative monitoring. Many people find it difficult to establish hard objectives in this way. But, with practice and some guidance from others who may be more experienced, most leaders and trainers find that outcomes can be defined for even the most complex tasks.

Evaluation Forms

42

Purpose   The prewritten evaluation form is a structured way of gathering information from all participants after an event. Findings can be collated and summarized in an evaluation report. At best, evaluation forms can be read and understood by people who were not part of the group.

Method   Draw up an evaluation sheet containing questions relevant to the program being evaluated. Copy and distribute to all participants. Forms can be completed towards the end of the event (ensuring a high return rate but without the opportunity for reflection) or mailed back later (after any euphoria about the event has subsided, yet running the risk that participants by then may be too busy to reply).

Evaluation sheets may take many forms: short or long; quantitative or qualitative; personal or anonymous; process-oriented or outcome-oriented. An example of a standard short-course evaluation form is given on the next page as a template.

Suitability   The value of evaluation forms depends on the degree of care participants take in their completion. If done in a hurry, the evaluations may be no more than impressionistic — and hardly worth collecting. Large numbers of short forms are probably only useful for producing data for summary reports about a wide-ranging program for many participants. A few well-considered evaluation forms are of far more use to the trainer or leader who wants to know how it felt to take the course, and how it might be improved if it were to be repeated.

WORKSHEET Evaluation Form

Your views and reactions to this event are welcomed. We aim to improve the effectiveness of what we do by learning from each participant's experience. Please take a few minutes to complete this form.

Name of event _____ **Date of event** _____

Your name _____

What were your goals in attending this event?

_____

_____

To what extent do you think each of these goals has been met?

_____

_____

What comments would you like to make, if any, about each of the following aspects of the event?

Location_____

Leader/trainer_____

Content _____

Style and format _____

Administration _____

Cost_____

What aspects would you highlight as being particularly effective or useful?

_____

_____

How might aspects be changed or improved?

_____

_____

What action do you plan to take as a follow-up this event?

_____

_____

Thank you for contributing to the evaluation. Please return this form to your session leader.

Event Charts

43

Purpose   Event charts are a graphic means of collecting reactions, opinions and suggestions about an event from the whole group. People add their comments to those contributed previously by others.

Method   The trainer prepares a large sheet of paper, either by using a roll of kraft paper, or by joining several flipchart sheets together. A thick line is drawn along the length of the sheet. The line represents the history of the group or course. Significant events are marked with an "X" at intervals along the line, corresponding chronologically to the time when they occurred. A brief note identifying each event is written alongside.

Participants are given pens and asked to write their comments about the events on the sheet. Positive comments can be written above the line and criticisms below it. With several people writing simultaneously at different points on the chart, it is probable that the comments from one person will trigger reactions from another, which are added to the chart.

When everyone has finished, the group is given time to study the final chart. A plenary discussion may then be held to consider the evaluation.

Possible variations   The chart can be made into a descriptive mural or collage by adding photographs or practical examples of the work of the group.

Suitability   This evaluation technique works well with self-help projects and in other groups in which there has been a strong sense of achievement and change.

Feedback Rounds

44

Purpose Rounds provide a quick method for gathering an instant reaction from all participants regarding the current state of the course or group.

Method At a suitable point in the program—usually at a natural break, between exercises or before moving on to a new topic—the trainer announces that she would like to hear from everyone how the course (or the most recent part of it) is going. The idea is to receive quick, impressionistic responses, not detailed, analytical answers. The "rules" of any feedback round are:

- Each person will have an opportunity to respond in turn.
- Each person will be listened to respectfully.
- Comments should be honest and constructive; the purpose is to comment on the group event, not assess or judge the person speaking.
- There will be no discussion about each person's contribution.
- If discussion is necessary, it will occur at the end of the round, after everyone has spoken.

In a feedback round, the trainer needs to devise a suitable question to which everyone is asked to respond. Avoid questions that could be answered with merely "yes" or "no". The question should be simple and straightforward:

"How do you feel about the course so far?"

"How comfortable do you feel with our work together in this group?"

"What do you think of this morning's work?"

"What was the best or worst part of this session?"

Having explained the round and given each person a minute or so to form a response, the trainer asks the first person to start the round. If necessary, the trainer will need to move the round on to the next person if one participant is getting into a lengthy response.

Depending on the replies, the trainer will need to assess at the end of the round if there is a need to discuss the outcome of the feedback or to change the nature of the group's work. Clearly, the more critical the feedback, the more important it is for the trainer to find ways of responding to it in the way the course or group is led.

Goodbyes. . .

Possible variations   One problem in rounds is that some participants can launch into lengthy answers that take too much time and may inhibit others. To avoid this, the trainer can ask for the response in the form of a simple score:

> "On a scale of zero to 10 (where zero is very low and 10 is very high), how would you rate the relevance of our session today to your work?"

This type of feedback round provides an instant picture, although the details may need to be teased out in a subsequent discussion.

Further examples of **Rounds** are provided in Chapter 3 (page 115).

Suitability   Rounds are simple and easy to use, provide almost-instant feedback, involve everyone and can be used with any group.

Goodbyes

45

Purpose   This exercise combines personal evaluations of an event with an opportunity to complete it by saying "goodbye" to the other participants. It uses the "coffee-break" method (see **Icebreakers,** page 77) to involve all participants in the dialogue.

Method   The group breaks into pairs, with partners facing each other in two lines down the length of the room. The trainer announces the subject to be discussed between the partners either as a question or as a sentence stem to be completed. Each pair responds to the topic by engaging in a quick conversation. Because all the pairs are speaking simultaneously, the exercise can be very noisy. Conversations last no longer than a minute. At the end of the minute, the trainer reminds each person to say goodbye to their current partner and then to change seats. Everyone stands and moves one chair to the left (those at the end of a row move to the start of the next row; a single odd number can sit out or participate from the top of the row). Everyone should now have a new pair partner. The trainer announces a new topic and the one-minute conversations are continued with the new partner. These goodbyes, moves and short dialogues are repeated until all participants have had a chance to speak to everyone else as they move around the chairs.

This technique becomes an evaluation and farewell exercise according to the nature of the questions or sentence stems provided by the trainer. A series of questions can be built up, starting with relatively easy ones and ending with more personal ones, to help participants express to each other what they have derived from working together. Such a series of sentence stems might include, for example:

"Something I wanted to gain from this course was. . . "

"The most interesting part of our work together has been. . . "

"The thing I will remember most from our group is. . . "

"The most difficult part of our work was. . . "

"If I were starting this group again, the thing I would do differently is. . . "

"If our group were made into a book or movie, it would be called. . . "

"Something I learned here was. . . "

"Something I learned about myself was. . . "

"Something I learned about you was. . . "

"An improvement I would suggest for this course is. . . "

"Before I go, I would like to say to you. . . "

Possible variations   Participants, rather than the trainer, can devise their own questions or sentence stems. In this case, the participant sitting at the end of the row can be given the responsibility (this person will change as people move from chair to chair). This method also enables the trainer to take part in the exercise as a participant and say "goodbye" to each person in turn.

Suitability   This is a participative exercise and works well for groups and courses that have had a high level of engagement. Because it enables people to mention anything about the course that may be incomplete for them, it can be of great help in bringing events to a clear conclusion and in facilitating departure.

Group Discussion

46

Purpose   This is the simplest method of gathering feedback from any group, requiring no preparation or forethought. It can be used at any time.

Method   This technique involves no more than stopping the group at some point and asking for comments and reactions from participants about how it is going (or some other relevant question). The trainer should be as neutral as possible, explaining that he is interested in people's feelings, does not anticipate any great problem and is simply giving participants an opportunity to say anything that might be important or bothersome to them at that moment.

Of course, if the trainer senses there is a problem or issue in the group that has not been expressed so far, it is quite legitimate for the trainer to mention this:

> "I sense some people are not happy with what we are doing just now. Can I ask you to stop for a few minutes and let me know how you are feeling about this task?"

As with any feedback exercise, it is the responsibility of the trainer or leader to consider how to respond to the comments and suggestions that are made and whether changes should be made in the program or process of the group.

Suitability   Short discussions about progress should be a common feature of all courses and group events so participants feel encouraged to contribute their views and deal with difficulties whenever they occur (and not just when feedback is asked for deliberately). This gives participants a greater sense of control over their own involvement.

Notes and Memos

47

Purpose   This is an effective, unstructured technique for gathering feedback from participants during periods of reflection between sessions.

Method   At the end of a session, or during a break between different parts of the group's program, the leader asks participants if they would be willing to reflect on the work of the group so far and to provide the leader with some feedback.

Each person is given paper or a memo pad. During an interval in the program, they are asked to compose a note to be given to the group leader. The note should give direct feedback to the leader about how the event is going from the viewpoint of the writer. The group leader may want to suggest some headings or give examples of the sort of feedback expected, but with adult groups this is rarely necessary. An unstructured request permits the participants to respond in individual ways and usually gives a strong qualitative "feel" to the feedback.

As with other feedback techniques, the leader can choose whether notes should be signed or not. If the participant expects a response from the leader to issues raised in the note, a name is necessary; if the leader anticipates receiving feedback of a critical nature, this may be more forthcoming if replies can be left unsigned.

Having collected the notes or memos, the leader will require time to read them and consider how to respond.

Possible variations   See **Diaries and Logs** in Chapter 3 (page 53) for other uses of unstructured writing exercises.

Suitability   This technique requires substantial breaks between sessions, when reflection and note writing can occur. It is particularly appropriate as a piece of overnight homework during a multi-day course, or as a task between sessions for a group that meets on, say, a weekly basis.

Score Charts

48

Purpose A score chart is a graphic way of showing reactions to an event on a prepared chart. The chart is usually quick to complete and easy to interpret. The results from score charts completed by several participants can be presented quantitatively for a more statistical approach to evaluation.

Method The trainer prepares a series of feedback questions that can be answered on some kind of linear scale, rather than in the simpler Yes/No format. Each question is written on a feedback sheet and followed by a rating scale (two polar opposites shown at either end and some interval marks between). The feedback sheet may consist of six questions. The feedback sheets are copied and distributed to each participant.

Examples of the technique A typical question and rating scale might be:

"To what extent is this course meeting your expectations?"

```
Very                                                              Very
poorly  |------+------+------+------+------|                      well
```

Some other questions capable of being answered by means of score charts include:

"How relevant is this course to your work?" (Very – Not at all)

"How much are you enjoying this session?" (A lot – Not very much)

"How are you finding the pace of this work?" (Too fast – Too slow)

"What do you think of the way we are working together?" (Too much input by trainer – Too much work by participants)

Some trainers prefer to add an open question at the end without a rating scale asking, "What other suggestions or comments would you like to make?"

When the score charts have been completed, collect them and consider what is revealed by the responses before deciding whether any changes are desirable.

Score Charts. . .

Possible variations

The score charts can be provided in different forms, such as a numbered scale (say from one to 10), or as check boxes.

By using a series of identical score charts at intervals throughout a long program or series of sessions, the dynamic impression of change in the group's reactions over time can be shown. The **Three-test Approach** (page 179) offers a further refinement, where rating scales can be used to measure change.

Suitability

Score charts can be introduced quickly. They do not take long to prepare. Answers can be signed or anonymous, depending on circumstances. Because the exercise relies on easily understood graphical methods, it can be completed by groups of all ages and literacy levels.

SWOT Analysis

49

Purpose   Although not technically a feedback or evaluation technique, SWOT analysis can provide a helpful method of reviewing the learning derived from a group or course. The technique is used most commonly in organizational reviews to assess the current position or status of the organization. With some amendments, it is offered here in a form that encourages discussion and reflection about a learning event.

Method   SWOT stands for *Strengths, Weaknesses, Opportunities* and *Threats*. These four headings provide a structured way of reviewing any group or event if interpreted as follows:

Strengths
What are we good at? What have we gained? Where are we confident?

Weaknesses
Where are we vulnerable? What else do we need to do or learn?

Opportunities
How will we now use what we have learned, gained or done?

Threats
What might undermine this learning? What support is required to make sure our plans happen?

Another way of considering this technique is that Strengths and Weaknesses can refer to the internal events of the group or event and Opportunities and Threats relate to external factors affecting them.

The technique works best when participants work in small groups, each with a poster-sized version of the SWOT grid (see example on page 176). They then complete each quadrant of the grid with their ideas. The finished grids can be displayed, compared and discussed.

Suitability   SWOT analysis is a straightforward exercise to introduce. It is easy to understand, particularly as many people have come across the method before in other contexts. The presentation of results on poster-size sheets makes for easy display and comparison, and provides clear visual feedback about the learning.

SWOT Analysis Chart – Examples

STRENGTHS

What are we good at?

What have we gained?

Where are we confident?

WEAKNESSES

Where are we vulnerable?

What else do we need
to do or learn?

OPPORTUNITIES

How will we now use what
we have learned, gained
or done?

THREATS

What might undermine
this learning?

What support is required to make
sure our plans happen?

Talking Wall

50

Purpose   The talking wall is a group exercise that provides opportunities for all participants to evaluate the event by responding to open questions or statements from the trainer. The exercise is conducted so all comments are public for others to read and add to in an interactive way.

Method   Several flipchart sheets are prepared as posters by the trainer in advance. Each poster contains an open statement printed at the top. Typical statement stems might include:

> "The best part of this course for me was. . ."
>
> "The worst part of this course for me was. . ."
>
> "This course could be improved by. . ."
>
> "If I were doing this course again, I would. . ."
>
> "When I first arrived here, I felt. . ."
>
> "As I am leaving, I feel. . ."
>
> "Something I learned here is. . ."
>
> "A surprise for me was. . ."
>
> "The thing I will take from this course and use most is. . ."

Ideally, prepare 10 such posters. Place them around the wall of the room where everyone can read them. Give each participant a marker pen and invite them to walk around the room adding appropriate comments to each sheet. Alternatively, give each person a supply of adhesive memo pads and a pencil. Ask them to write comments on separate stickers and post them on the most appropriate sheet. Encourage everyone to read the comments written by others.

Possible variations   A shortened version of this exercise is to use three posters headed: "Positive Comments," "Negative Comments" and "Interesting Comments" (the latter comprising comments and suggestions that do not fit neatly into the positive or negative comment categories). Participants either write on the sheets themselves, or the trainer completes them as a brainstorm session with the group.

A different way of using such questions or statements is provided in the **Goodbyes** exercise (page 167).

Suitability   This technique is thought-provoking and fun to do for virtually all groups.

Three-test Approach

51

Purpose   The three-test approach uses rating scales applied on three occasions to measure the degree of before-and-after change in the knowledge or skills of participants. Although not completely objective, it provides a quantifiable method of assessing how much change has occurred as a consequence of the learning event.

Method   A questionnaire or evaluation sheet is prepared that lists a series of knowledge areas, skills or behaviors relevant to the course or event. Each of these is accompanied by a rating scale. Participants complete a self-assessment of their knowledge, skill or behavior on three separate occasions using identical copies of the sheet:

The first sheet is completed before or at the start of the event to record the initial rating.

The second sheet is completed at the end of the event to show the change in perceived ratings over the event.

The third sheet is also completed at the end of the event but with a different instruction to participants. They should indicate their revised assessment of their pre-event scoring on the basis of what they now know or understand about each factor, having completed the event.

The comparison of the first and second scores gives a false impression of the degree of change achieved by the event because the participants' knowledge or skill base has changed as a result of participation in the course itself. The two are not comparable. The third sheet provides a revised assessment of how much each participant knew or was capable of at the outset, based upon her greater understanding of the subject at the end. The second and third sheet scores *are* comparable because they are based on the *same amount* of knowledge. A truer reflection of perceived change is provided by the comparison of the third and second sheets. With numerical rating scales, this change can be calculated and shown graphically.

Possible variations   Instead of issuing three rating sheets, some groups manage with the same rating sheet, issued on three occasions with separate columns for each score. This requires clear instructions to participants about how and when to complete each column. A template for such a form is provided on page 180.

Suitability   The three-test approach can be a more difficult evaluation method to explain, so you may want to restrict it to adult audiences where a measurement of the degree of change is required. The technique is not completely objective because it relies upon participants' self-assessments. This means that the results may not be comparable among participants; neither do they necessarily score knowledge and skills against any objective "maximum".

Three-test Rating Scale – Template

Instruction to Participants

For each of the subjects in the list below, please score your own assessment of your knowledge, skills or awareness. Each subject should be given a score from **0** to **10**, where **0** indicates no knowledge or a total absence of skill and **10** indicates complete knowledge or skill ability.

Complete the first column at the start of the course.

Complete the second column at the end of the course.

At the end of the course, use the knowledge and skill you gained during the course to revise your self-assessment of your precourse knowledge or skill. Record your revised assessment in the third column. The difference between scores in columns 3 and 2 shows the degree of change.

	1 Initial score	2 Terminal score	3 Revised initial	4 Degree of change score (2 minus 3)
First knowledge area				
Second knowledge area				
Third knowledge area				
Fourth knowledge area				
First skill ability				
Second skill ability				
Third skill ability				
Fourth skill ability				

Chapter 5
Tools for Coworking

Trainers and group leaders often spend much of their time working alone. This gives them sole responsibility for the course or event and the freedom to plan and deliver it in their own way. They do not have to consult with others about the style or content at the planning stage and, when training or leading, the solo trainer is in complete control.

Working on your own with a group has several disadvantages. It can be an unsupported situation, particularly for the trainer who is not part of a larger team. The lack of support may be most evident when matters are not going well. If the course is slow or the group is resistant, there are no colleagues with whom to discuss problems, or who can help you devise solutions.

A coworker is a partner who shares the tasks, problems and successes of the group and provides support and a sounding board throughout the event.

While coworkers may often be regarded as equal partners in the process, this may not be so. One partner may be senior to the other (for instance, where one partner is more experienced or supervises the other). This form of "learning by supporting" can be effective for a less experienced trainer or group worker in acquiring skills and insights from a mentor.

Effective coworking does not just happen automatically when two people are in the same room together. Any two trainers will probably have different styles, different preferences in how they establish relations with participants, different tolerance levels and differences in their favorite techniques and methods. The essence of good coworking is that these differences can be recognized and harnessed to provide a more effective learning environment for the participants. To do this, the two leaders who are to work together must spend time together. They need to share their approaches and recognize the particular strengths and contributions of the other.

This chapter describes several useful activities that can be used by potential coworkers in their preparation. Each activity aims to create a dialog between the coworkers through which they can explore their respective styles and methods. As with many other techniques, it is the nature and quality of this conversation that is important, rather than any slavish adherence to the mechanics of the exercise.

Coworking Dialog

52

Purpose   This technique uses the **Dialog Book** approach (page 51) to structure a conversation between two prospective coworkers about their respective styles, methods and goals. The exercise can be changed and extended by the addition of other questions.

Method   Trainers work in pairs, each with a prospective coworker. Each person has a copy of the coworking dialog questions. These can be listed (as they are on the example on the next page) or written on separate cards in order. The latter method has the benefit of preventing participants from looking ahead.

The pair takes each question in turn and in the order given. Each person responds to each of the questions. It does not matter who goes first — this is likely to vary as the exercise proceeds. Take as long as necessary to answer each question. Encourage opportunities to explore issues raised by the question. The questions are deliberately open-ended to facilitate such discussion. One or the other partner may decline to answer a question without explanation for personal reasons if necessary.

At the end of the exercise, partners should review what they have learned about each other and about the opportunities available for working together.

Coworking Dialog Questions

1. My experience in training and running a group includes. . .

2. An example of a successful event I have run recently is. . .

3. I believe that people are helped to learn by. . .

4. My strengths as a trainer and group leader include. . .

5. Some things that other people have said about my abilities as a trainer are. . .

6. My favorite techniques are. . .

7. Some techniques I am less experienced or confident in are. . .

8. As a trainer, what I am trying to achieve is. . .

9. Something I would like to do differently in my leadership role is. . .

10. This conversation is showing me that you and I differ in. . .

11. Some of my weaknesses as a trainer are. . .

12. The way in which I deal with problems in a group is. . .

13. When I feel uncertain in my training role, I. . .

14. By our working together, I am looking for. . .

15. I like to support others by. . .

16. What I am learning about your approach is. . .

17. Something else you should know about me is. . .

18. What I most value about coworking is. . .

Tool Kit for Trainers

Leadership Rating

53

Purpose This technique invites coworkers to use self-rating scales as a way of assessing and describing their own approach and skills in various aspects of training and group leadership. Completed scales can be compared and discussed as a prelude to any joint planning and training.

Method Each person independently completes one of the leadership rating scales using scores from one (low) to five (high) on each of the statements provided. See the worksheet on page 186 for examples.

At a suitable time, coworkers get together to compare their different rating scales and discuss the differences among them. As with all rating scales, the results are not strictly comparable because each person uses different norms when completing such self-assessments. Nevertheless, the sheets provide a useful starting point for any discussion of respective differences and potential pitfalls in working together.

During the discussion, coworkers should examine differences in style and approach, how these can be used to complement each other, and where conflict points might emerge. Ground rules for dealing with these need to be agreed before partnership working commences with participants for real.

Possible variations Standardized rating scales are often of limited use. It may be better for users to design their own, more-appropriate rating-scale statements. You may use the example on the following page as a starting point and add other statements relevant to your particular situation.

Some people dislike the five-point rating scores and prefer to choose from among three options for each statement:

- I'm happy with my present performance on this point.

- I need to do more of this.

- I need to do less of this.

Leadership Rating Scales

For each of the following statements, rank yourself on the scale from **1** to **5**.

	Low				High
My ability to plan and prepare materials	1	2	3	4	5
My knowledge of the subject matter	1	2	3	4	5
My skill in communicating with participants	1	2	3	4	5
My adaptability to change when circumstances require it	1	2	3	4	5
My ability to admit my own mistakes to others	1	2	3	4	5
My need to be in control of events	1	2	3	4	5
My tolerance of differences in others	1	2	3	4	5
My skill in creating a safe learning environment	1	2	3	4	5
My willingness to learn from others	1	2	3	4	5
My need to complete what I have planned	1	2	3	4	5
My sensitivity to difficulties experienced by others	1	2	3	4	5
My awareness of time	1	2	3	4	5
My ability to explain myself clearly	1	2	3	4	5
My willingness to let participants take increasing control	1	2	3	4	5
My ability to "think on my feet" and create alternatives	1	2	3	4	5
My willingness to try different approaches	1	2	3	4	5
My awareness of my own limits	1	2	3	4	5

Tool Kit for Trainers

Message Sheets

54

Purpose   Sometimes coworkers start to work together without realizing the differences between them. One or more incidents may prompt a review of the working arrangements. At this stage, making clear requests to a partner can be awkward because the task has to continue despite the difficulties. Message sheets are a way of giving clear feedback about the support each person needs from the other.

Participant risk factor **3**

Method   Coworkers need to recognize that difficulties exist between them before using the exercise. Each person completes one or more message sheets (use more than one if several people are working together). Complete the message sheets honestly and directly. Do not add justifications or explanations, as these often confuse the original message. If any are required, add them verbally later.

Each person hands his message sheet(s) to the intended recipient(s). In the pair discussions that follow, message sheets can be clarified where necessary and agreements made between coworkers about how they will work together in future.

Message Sheet

This message is from _____

This message is to _____

I suggest we could work together better if_____

_____

_____

_____

_____

_____

You could do the following things differently_____

_____

_____

_____

_____

I could start doing the following differently_____

_____

_____

_____

_____

You could support me by _____

_____

_____

_____

_____

_____

We could clear up the following areas of difficulty together_____

_____

_____

_____

_____

_____

Tool Kit for Trainers

Pen Pictures

55

Purpose

This exercise uses drawing to encourage each person to express self-perceptions about personal leadership skills. The pictures are used as the basis for discussion between coworkers. The level of interpretation given to each picture can be as simple or complex as you wish.

Method

Each person takes a large sheet of paper and several pens or markers. Working individually, each person draws a picture, diagram or outline of himself on the front of the sheet, illustrating his skills, abilities and strengths as a group leader or trainer. The illustrations should rely on drawings rather than words on the paper, but drawing skills are not to be assessed.

When each person has completed his drawing, prospective coworkers get together in pairs to explain and discuss their drawings. The focus is on gaining an understanding of each other's strengths and abilities when training. Questions are encouraged as a way of extending the discussion.

Each pair concludes the exercise by listing any points they need to take into account about each other when planning or working together. These may form ground rules for their joint work.

Possible variations

As well as depicting strengths, the method can be used to illustrate respective areas of weakness, lack of confidence or inexperience. The exercise can be extended by asking each person to use the reverse side of his sheet of paper (or use the same side but in a different color ink) to draw a second picture showing these aspects.

Where partners know each other reasonably well before the pen pictures are drawn, they can be encouraged to add material to each other's illustrations during the discussion stage using Post-It® notes or cards to represent points they feel were inadequately recognized in the original drawing.

Styles Questionnaire

56

Purpose   This exercise helps two or more trainers prepare to work together, perhaps for the first time. The styles questionnaire highlights a number of preferences about the approach that each trainer adopts when working with a group. Many trainers are so familiar and comfortable with their own approach that they may forget that others work in different ways. Completion of this exercise in advance makes trainers aware of their different preferences. With it, they can discuss their approaches openly and make informed decisions about the desirability of coworking and the roles each might play with the group.

Method   Working individually, each trainer completes the styles questionnaire. (See the following page for some examples of areas that a styles questionnaire might cover.) They meet to compare the results. This will lead to debate about what each trainer means by particular responses; specific examples may be discussed. Areas of particular overlap and divergence should be examined closely, so the trainers can plan ahead for their respective roles when such situations arise in practice.

Styles Questionnaire

Think about each of the following pairs of statements in turn in relation to your recent work with training groups. Mark with an "X" on the line the point that most closely reflects your own preferred style.

Demonstrate that I always have an answer for each question	————————	Let participants see that there are considerable gaps in my own knowledge and experience
Open to alternative ideas and suggestions, even when I don't agree with them	————————	Critical of other people's ideas if I don't agree with them
Use humor and diversion as a helpful aid	————————	Maintain a clear focus on the point
Avoid situations in which stress and conflict may arise	————————	Allow conflict to arise and deal with it as necessary
Nondirective	————————	Directive
Allow other people to know personal information about me	————————	Keep my personal life and affairs separate
Maintain the focus on the task of the group	————————	Allocate time to relationship and other difficulties at the expense of the task if this seems appropriate
Allow people to make their own decisions, even if I don't agree	————————	Attempt to change people's decisions and actions to what I think is right
Avoid risks	————————	Take risks
Allow the group to take increasing control	————————	Maintain my authority
Stick to the agenda	————————	Explore topics off the agenda if they arise

Tool Kit for Trainers

Chapter 6

Tools for Coping with Problems

P roblems and difficulties can be expected when working with almost any training and learning group. There are many reasons for this. As the work of most groups is concerned with developing and moving on, an element of change is implicit. Yet change itself is often threatening and generates resistance and barriers among those who are involved. To overcome these problems, the group leader must be able to recognize and respond to difficulties in an effective manner. This chapter is concerned with extending the group worker's tool kit for handling such problems.

The trainer or group leader needs to develop expertise in handling problems in three areas:

- planning ahead to prepare contingency methods;
- recognizing and dealing with resistance; and
- building confidence in working with any group.

Developing confidence comes with experience and success. There is no shortcut to getting involved in training and running groups, and finding out for yourself what can happen and how you should respond. For those who are relatively inexperienced, there are inevitably anxieties about coping with difficulties. This is because, in the heat of the moment, when all eyes are on you as the "performer" responsible for the event, it is all too easy to forget the best-made plans and fall into the traps that surround you. Such occasions are perhaps inevitable. Yet they also provide some of the best learning opportunities for anyone running training and learning groups, provided time is given to proper reflection and understanding of these occasions. These pages of the *Tool Kit* may help you debrief such events.

More tips and tactics both for contingency planning and for handling resistance are explored in this chapter.

Contingency Planning

57

Purpose Contingency planning is any method you may use to prepare your reactions and responses to an unforeseen or unwanted event. A contingency plan provides a "fallback" option if what you are currently doing does not work.

Method Contingency plans may be formally or informally arranged. A formal plan entails devising an alternative exercise or method to be used at each stage of the planned program. Formal contingency plans provide security for the trainer, who is reassured by the knowledge that alternatives exist. However, such security may be false. Formal contingency plans are often inflexible. Because they are prepared in advance, they cannot take into account what actually happens during the event. They are unlikely to cover every eventuality.

Informal contingency plans are made up and revised at each stage of the event as the planned program progresses. They are adaptable to what is happening and take into account the reactions and responses of the group. They rely on the quick thinking and creativity of the trainer to invent alternative methods and plans at each stage. For some, this is "flying by the seat of your pants."

Informal contingency planning works best if the trainer can keep three plans in her head at any one time:

- what is happening now as part of the program;

- what is planned to happen next, or will be introduced if the present activity does not work; and

- what to do if that fails also.

This may seem like extreme contingency planning, and overdemanding in preparation, but it need not be. The first plan, the program itself, is already under way. The second plan is likely to be the next part of the intended program—where the present event is designed to lead. The third plan is a fallback option if the program goes seriously wrong.

Keeping these three plans in your head doesn't have to be difficult. It requires you to monitor the work of the group at regular intervals, assess progress against the planned program, and to update the contingency plans as you go along.

Examples of the technique

To illustrate the use of contingency planning, here are some common ways of working out alternatives. One of the easiest to remember is the notion of **working with opposites** (fully explained in Chapter 2). Briefly, working with opposites suggests that if what you are now doing with the group is not working, switch to its opposite.

- If a plenary session is not working, break into smaller groups.
- If a practical exercise is not working, change it to a demonstration.
- If a thinking session is not working, move on to a practical activity.
- If you are heavily engaged in process, switch to a task.
- If a trainer example is not working, seek out a participant example.

Another way of planning contingencies is to develop a series of simple activities or exercises that can be relied upon to help resolve the most common problems encountered with any group. Use them as necessary when the problem arises.

- If participants stop paying attention to the content, divide them into smaller groups and ask them to apply the material to situations from their own experience.
- If you are unsure what to do next, announce a break for refreshments to give yourself time to think.
- If there seems to be resistance in the group, call for a round in which people express how they are feeling (see **Feedback Rounds**, page 165).
- If the present session is running out of steam, move on to the next part of the program early.
- If you are running out of material, end the session early rather than create fillers.
- If the group is becoming fragmented, bring participants together and ask them to work on clarifying the purpose of their common work.

Many of these common contingencies rely upon the use of opposites. They also generate space either for the trainer to reassert a measure of control or for participants to express their own difficulties in a legitimate way within the group.

Detecting Resistance

58

Purpose   This section summarizes the two most reliable methods of knowing when the behavior or actions of another person constitute "resistance". One method relies upon an intuitive sense, the other upon more rational analysis.

Method   Perhaps the simplest way of detecting resistance is to rely upon your subjective sense of when a situation is "right" or "wrong". Provided the trainer can retain at least an element of detachment from the situation and monitor what is happening within the group, the intuitive "feel" for the group will come into play. With experience, most trainers come to rely upon this intuitive sense for assessing their groups.

How does the intuitive sense manifest itself? Usually with a thought or "gut feeling" that something is not quite right. When asked to pin this down, many trainers find difficulty because the evidence is inferential and circumstantial. Clues might include quiet whispering among participants, a general reluctance to participate, a sense of hostility or resentment, difficult communication, the nonverbal signals emitted by participants, poor timekeeping, avoidance of the subject, and so on. None of these clues *alone* indicates resistance. However, these clues in context may lead the trainer to sense that something is amiss.

In more than 95% of occasions where the trainer senses a problem, there is one. Nineteen out of 20 is not a bad prediction rate! An intuitive feeling of something being wrong is an accurate basis on which to act. Even if the trainer does not know what the problem is, or what to do about it, recognizing the existence of a difficulty is a critical first step.

A more rational approach to detecting resistance (which can also build upon the first intuitive sense) is provided by the "rule of three". This works as follows:

- The *first* time something unexpected happens, accept it at face value and give a response in good faith. The unexpected event may be an interruption, question, challenge, breaking of a ground rule, or whatever. It is accepted and dealt with fully and properly.

- The *second* time the same (or similar) unexpected event happens, accept it, too, at face value, provide a good-faith response—but make a mental note that this is a second occurrence and may be the start of a pattern. Thus when a participant challenges for the second time, or a second distraction occurs, or a delay is introduced for the second time, accept it, respond as if it were the first occurrence, but note the repetition to yourself.

- The *third* time the same (or similar) unexpected event happens, it is resistance. Rather than responding in the same way as for the first and second occurrence, deal with the resistance itself (see **Confronting Resistance,** page 201).

The rule-of-three test provides a reliable method for detecting resistance. It does not require the same resistance to recur each time, but it searches for patterns. A pattern may be the same participant generating difficulties on each occasion, or a small group of participants regularly asking the same sort of question. The rule of three provides a way of knowing when to stop responding in good faith, and when to start confronting the resistance itself.

Several examples of different forms of resistance are provided on the accompanying handout (pages 199-200) to help you detect such problems.

Examples of the technique

A trainer working with staff on a communication-skills course over two days became aware of a difficulty in the group. During the first morning, two participants kept at a distance and did not seem to take part with the others; they whispered to each other but did not talk to the trainer. She decided to use the rule of three to confirm her impression that there was a problem.

The trainer set the group to work on an exercise. The two participants causing concern were slow to get going and produced little work. The trainer helped them complete the task. At the start of the afternoon session, the same two participants were the only people back late from the lunch break. The trainer pointed this out and asked them to observe the agreement about start times. Half an hour later, during another exercise, the trainer noticed the same two participants were not carrying out the task and were managing to distract several others. The trainer felt her initial awareness of a problem had been confirmed and that now was the time to act. She was pretty sure neither of these participants had any commitment to the course.

When participants resist what is happening in a group, it achieves one of two outcomes:

- it exerts their control over the process; or

- it defends their weaknesses in the process.

The entries below describe common ways in which participants may demonstrate their resistance to what is happening in the group. Taken individually, such behavior is not necessarily resistance. Much depends on the context in which the behavior occurs and the participant's motive for using it. A pattern of such behavior tends to confirm the presence of resistance (but beware of stereotyping people who are expressing difficulty with the topic or process of the group).

Competition

This form of resistance is shown by someone who may feel anxious to demonstrate that his knowledge or experience is more extensive, more detailed or more relevant than that of the trainer or the other participants. The competitor's constant interruptions to recount his examples become frustrating for everyone else.

Challenge

This is a particular form of competition. The person is so convinced by his own examples and ideas that he challenges for the leadership of the group. This may take the form of a direct challenge to the trainer, or it may be a more subtle gathering of support among participants to create an alternative power grouping within the event. Alternative leaders tend to question and attack the group leader in an attempt to weaken the leader's position. In even more extreme situations they may refuse to carry out a task and provoke a direct confrontation.

Drifting

This describes someone who follows the ideas and suggestions of others. She fails or refuses to supply her own ideas and initiative. The problem may be a lack of confidence or assertiveness. It may also be an unwillingness to make an effort, preferring to rely on the work of others instead.

Continued. . .

Forms of Resistance Handout/continued

Sabotage

Saboteurs act from within the group to undermine the group process. On the surface, the saboteur appears as a cooperative participant, yet underneath he is deliberately finding ways to disrupt the group. This disruption may take many forms. Some of the most common forms of sabotage are:

- ignoring or breaking the ground rules;

- creating red herrings that divert energy and attention from the group's purpose;

- asking questions that challenge the knowledge or competence of the trainer;

- setting up other group processes within the event that undermine the group's functioning; and

- initiating tasks different than those requested by the group's leaders.

Silence

This is one of the most difficult forms of resistance to deal with. A silent participant gives few clues to the cause of the problem. Yet the longer someone remains silent, the greater the obstacle she poses to the rest of the group or to any attempt at inclusion. Remaining silent can be a most powerful way of attracting attention.

Thinking

This resistance is seen in someone who insists on thinking about and "processing" everything that is said or done. Rather than engaging in a practical way in what is happening, the thinker will sit out and consider it, preferring to "work it out" is his head. This tactic avoids the emotional and physical aspects of any event and provides a form of defense to participants who are less confident.

Acting

This behavior is almost the reverse of thinking. The person will accept all instructions and endeavor to carry them out as quickly as possible, usually without giving any time to preparation or thinking. This tactic demonstrates the person's commitment to the task but also covers up a lack of understanding or an anxiety about getting it right.

Scapegoating

In some groups, a weaker (or absent) person becomes the scapegoat for others who need someone to blame. However, scapegoats can be self-created when a participant wishes to attract attention or be seen as some sort of victim of circumstance. By becoming a scapegoat, the person avoids accepting responsibility for what is happening.

Confronting Resistance

59

Purpose   Handling resistance is often one of the most difficult roles for trainers or group leaders, because they feel responsible for solving the resistance. Many group leaders would rather put up with the disruption caused by the resistance than deal with it directly. Such a view places responsibility for resistance in the wrong camp. The difficulty or resistance is experienced by one or more participants in the group — it is *they* who need encouragement and support to accept their responsibility in the matter and deal with the problem. For the trainer, confronting resistance should be just that — confronting it — and leaving the problem with the person causing it. When this has been accepted, both participant and trainer can work together on its resolution. This section provides one method for achieving this end.

Method   There are four steps to confronting resistance:

1. Identify the resistance

This step uses the methods from **Detecting Resistance** (page 197) to spot when resistance is occurring. The trainer must use his senses and experience to be 95% certain of the resistance and to be able to say what form it takes.

2. Name the resistance

The trainer is responsible for confronting the participant (or group) with the resistance. This is done by naming it — pointing out what is happening in as simple and neutral a way as possible. It is important not to attribute blame or judgment in the process. The trainer announces the presence of the resistance, asks for confirmation or agreement, and creates an opportunity for it to be dealt with openly by those present.

3. Remain silent

This is perhaps the hardest part of the process. Having named the resistance, the trainer should remain silent. No explanations, no justifications, no rationalizations. The course program will inevitably stop. Trainer and participants will feel under pressure because of the silence. If there is resistance, the participant(s) concerned will feel under greater pressure. By remaining silent, the trainer invites a response to her assertion and the naming of it.

4. Deal with the underlying problem and move on

Remember that all resistance stems either from the participant's need to exert his strength and control, or from his need to defend his weaknesses. The silence is designed to elicit a response. Having obtained a response, the trainer and participant together can work on the underlying cause of the problem. There is no standard formula for this because the problems will be specific to the situation. It remains for the participant and trainer to negotiate a resolution together. Once the underlying problem is resolved, the program can resume.

While this technique is the best-known method for confronting resistance, it is not infallible. During step 3, the participants may deny the problem or seek to explain away each piece of evidence offered by the trainer. Avoid being drawn into justifications; they are unproductive. Questioning your observations may be just another form of resistance. Rather than arguing over it, accept the denial and continue, while adding that denial to a further rule-of-three computation to be used in a later attempt at confronting the resistance. Of course, if you are genuinely mistaken (less than one occasion in 20), accept the correction, apologize in good faith and continue.

Possible variations The only alternative to confronting resistance is putting up with it. This is rarely a successful tactic: Contrary to our every wish, resistance does not go away of its own accord. It is easy to take resistance as a personal attack upon your competence. You may not be perfect, but it is of no help to anyone to personalize the issue in this way. To deflect such an attack, try to turn around the problem: "What can we do here and now to solve this problem?" Above all, in detecting resistance and confronting resistance, avoid dealing merely with the incidents: The incidents are evidence of the underlying problem—which is where action is required. The underlying cause is concerned with asserting control or defending weaknesses, and it is *these* issues that you will need to address with the participants or group.

Index

Notes

Notes